JN090730

英語
日本紹介事典
JAPAPEDIA

ジャパペディア

新版

IBCパブリッシング 編

IBCパブリッシング

編集協力＝松浦斉美
翻訳協力＝Ed Jacob
カバーデザイン＝岩目地英樹（コムデザイン）
イラスト＝テッド高橋　横井智美

まえがき

本書は、シンプルな例文によって、日本のさまざまな事情を紹介するフレーズブックです。日本をまるごとフレーズで分解した究極の日本紹介書ともいえるかもしれません。

日本を訪れる外国人の旅行客数は、コロナ禍を経て再び増加しています。2023年は年間で2500万人を突破し、コロナ禍前の8割近くまで回復しました。日本にいれば誰もが知っている観光名所、味や種類が豊富でおいしい食事はもちろん、日本人からすれば「なぜ？」と思うような地域や文物にまで、外国人たちの日本に対する興味は尽きません。そして彼らは、日本でのリアルな暮らしを知り、日本人と交流することを求めて、やって来るのです。こうした日本のさまざまな側面をどのように“英語で”紹介するかというテーマは、私たち日本人にとって永遠の課題でもあります。

どのように自分の故郷を説明するか。さらに、海外への出張や留学の際に、外国人から日本について聞かれたら、どう答えるか。また、海外からのお客さんを接待するときに、いかに日本のことを伝えるか。これらの課題に具体的な文例で応えるのが本書の狙いです。もちろん、海外へ手紙やメールを書くときの参考にもしていただければ幸いです。

本書で紹介する文章は、あくまでも参考です。出てくる例文やフレーズを参照しながら、自分なりに日本を紹介する方法をぜひ編み出していただきたいと思っています。ただ丸暗記するのではなく、固有名詞や単語を入れ替えるなどして、自分の言葉に直して使ってみてください。完璧である必要はありません。何度もチャレンジしていく中で、自らの個性に見合った表現で日本を伝えることができるようになるはずです。

外国人たちはあなたが語る言葉を待っています。本書を対話のきっかけとして、読者の皆さんと外国人の方々が互いを理解する一助となることを願っています。

IBC編集部一同

●音声ダウンロードについて●

本書の英語の音声ファイル(MP3形式)をダウンロードして聞くことができます。

各セクションの冒頭にあるQRコードをスマートフォンで読み取って、再生・ダウンロードしてください。音声ファイルはトピックごとに分割されていますので、お好きな箇所をくり返し聞いていただけます。

また、下記URLとQRコードからは音声ファイルを一括ダウンロードすることができます。

https://ibcpub.co.jp/audio_dl/0821/

※ ダウンロードしたファイルはZIP形式で圧縮されていますので、解凍ソフトが必要です。

※ MP3ファイルを再生するには、iTunes(Apple Music)やWindows Media Playerなどのアプリケーションが必要です。

※ PCや端末、ソフトウェアの操作・再生方法については、編集部ではお答えできません。付属のマニュアルやインターネットの検索を利用するか、開発元にお問い合わせください。

第1章

日本の基本情報

日本の基本情報

日本の地理・気候

日本の基本情報

「にっぽん」または「にほん」と読みます。どちらも多く用いられているため、日本政府は正式な読み方をどちらか一方には定めておらず、どちらの読みでも良いとしています。古くは「倭」と呼ばれました。

国名

□ 日本語では、日本のことをニッポンといいます。

□ ニッポンは日本の公式な名前です。

□ 日本人は時々、ニッポンをニホンと発音します。

暦・元号

□ 日本は西洋諸国と同じ太陽暦を使っています。

□ 旧暦とは太陰暦のことで、日本は1872年まで使っていました。

□ 日本では、西暦と日本式の元号の両方を使っています。たとえば、西暦2024年は、令和6年です。

□ 元号はもとは中国からきたものですが、今では日本独自の制度を使っています。

□ 日本の年号制度では、新たな天皇が皇位を継承してからの年数が基本になっています。

□ 2024年は日本式では令和6年です。現在の天皇が皇位を継承して6年目ということです。

民族・移民

□ 日本の人口の98%が日本人です。

□ 日本には、約6万3000人のアメリカ人が住んでいます。

Track 01

Country Name

In Japanese, Japan is called Nippon.

Nippon is the official name of Japan.

Japanese people sometimes pronounce Nippon as *Nihon*.

Calendars & *Gengo*

Japan uses the same solar calendar as Western countries.

Kyureki is the lunar calendar that Japan used until 1872.

In Japan, people use both the Western calendar and Japanese eras called *gengo*. For example, the year 2024 is also called Reiwa 6.

Gengo originally came from China, but Japan has its own era system.

The Japanese era system is based on the number of years after the new emperor succeeded to the throne.

The year 2024 is called Reiwa 6 in Japan. It means that six years have passed since the current Emperor succeeded to the throne.

Ethnicity & Immigration

In Japan, 98 percent of the population is Japanese.

There are about 63,000 American people living in Japan.

□ 日本に住んでいる外国人は299万人ほどです。

□ 北海道にはアイヌと呼ばれる先住民がいます。

□ 北海道にはアイヌと呼ばれる先住民がいて、その人口は約1万3000人です。

□ 2023年、日本を訪れた外国人はおよそ2500万人です。

□ 日本人と結婚して日本に住む外国人はおよそ20万人です。

□ 日本にいる留学生は約24万人です。

時間帯

□ 日本標準時はUTC（世界標準時）プラス9時間です。

□ 日本は、イギリスより9時間進んでいます（サマータイム時は8時間）。

□ 日本と韓国は同じ時間帯です。

単位

□ 日本では、1885年以来、メートル法を使っています。

□ 重さの単位にはグラムを、体積の単位にはリットルを使います。

□ 尺貫法とは、日本古来の計量法です。尺は長さの単位、貫は質量の単位です。

□ 日本の通貨は円です。

□ 日本の通貨は円で、換算レートは変動為替相場が基本になっています。

□ 銭と厘は、円のさらに下の単位ですが、紙幣や硬貨としては今では使われていません。

There are about 2.99 million foreigners living in Japan.

There are indigenous people called Ainu living in Hokkaido.

There are indigenous people called Ainu in Hokkaido, with a population of about 13,000.

In 2023, about 25 million foreigners visited Japan.

There are about 200,000 foreigners living in Japan who are married to Japanese.

The number of foreign students in Japan is about 240,000.

Time Zones

Japan Standard Time is UTC plus nine hours.

Japan is nine hours ahead of Britain (eight hours during daylight saving time).

Japan and Korea are in the same time zone.

Units of Measure

Japan has used the metric system since 1885.

Japan uses grams as units for measuring weight and liters as units for measuring volume.

Shakkanho is a traditional Japanese system of measurement. A *Shaku* is a unit of length and a *kan* is for measuring mass.

Japan's currency is the yen.

The Japanese currency is the yen, and the conversion rate is based on a floating exchange rate.

Sen and *rin* are amounts below one yen, but they are not used as notes and coins anymore.

交通・入国

□ 日本では車は左側通行です。

□ 主要空港は、東京近郊にある成田国際空港と、大阪周辺向けの関西国際空港です。

□ 東京周辺には、成田と羽田の国際空港があります。

□ 関西国際空港は、大阪周辺地区向けです。

□ 中部国際空港は、名古屋周辺地区向けです。

□ 北海道の新千歳空港と九州の福岡空港へは、国際線も乗り入れています。

成田空港

電話・インターネット

□ 日本の国際電話の国番号は81です。

□ たいていのホテルには、Wi-Fiが完備されています。

□ ネットカフェに行けば、インターネットにアクセスできる有料のパソコンが使えます。

□ 公共交通でもWi-Fiが利用できます。

Traffic and Entry

In Japan, cars drive on the left.

Major airports are Narita International Airport near Tokyo and Kansai International Airport near Osaka.

Narita and Haneda International Airports are located in the Tokyo area.

Kansai International Airport serves the Osaka area.

Chubu International Airport serves the Nagoya area.

International flights are also available from New Chitose Airport in Hokkaido and Fukuoka Airport in Kyushu.

羽田空港

Telephone and Internet

The international telephone code for Japan is 81.

Most hotels are equipped with Wi-Fi.

Internet cafés have computers that can be used to access the Internet for a fee.

Wi-Fi is also available on public transportation.

日本の地理・気候

日本の位置、地勢や気候を英語で説明できるようになりましょう。日本には四季があることや、夏は暑さの他に湿度が高いことなどを説明できるといいでしょう。

日本の位置

□ 日本は極東に位置しています。

□ 日本は極東の、アジアの端にあります。

□ 日本は極東に位置する島国です。

□ 日本の近隣諸国は、韓国、中国、ロシアなどです。

□ 日本は極東に位置しており、隣国は韓国、中国、ロシアです。

□ 日本海の向こうは、中国、ロシア、韓国です。

□ 日本とアジア諸国の間には、日本海があります。

□ 日本は太平洋を挟んで、アメリカと向き合っています。

□ 日本は環太平洋地域の国の一つです。

□ 東京からトロントまでの距離は1万300kmです。

□ トロントから東京までは飛行機でおよそ13時間かかります。

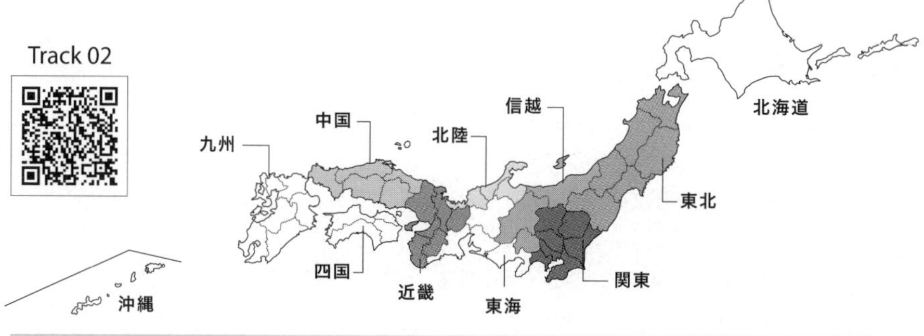

Location of Japan

Japan is located in the Far East.

Japan is located in the Far East, on the edge of Asia.

Japan is an island nation located in the Far East.

Japan's neighbors include South Korea, China, and Russia.

Japan is located in the Far East, and its neighbors are South Korea, China, and Russia.

Across the Sea of Japan are China, Russia, and Korea.

The Sea of Japan lies between Japan and other Asian countries.

Japan faces the United States across the Pacific Ocean.

Japan is one of the countries located along the Pacific rim.

The distance from Tokyo to Toronto is 10,300 km.

It takes approximately 13 hours to fly from Toronto to Tokyo.

日本のサイズ

□日本の国土はおよそ37万8000平方キロです。

□日本の国土は37万8000平方キロで、ドイツより少し大きいです。

□日本の国土は、アメリカ、中国、ロシアと比べると狭いです。

□日本の面積はスペインの4分の3です。

日本の国力

□日本は世界第４位の経済大国です。

□日本は先進国です。

□日本のインフラは高度に発展しています。

□日本の教育システムは進歩しています。

日本の治安

□日本は犯罪が少ないことで知られています。

□日本は犯罪が少ないことで知られています。統計によると、日本全体の犯罪発生件数は、カナダの15%程度です。

日本の人口

□日本の人口はおよそ1億2千万です。

□約1億2千万の人が日本には住んでいます。

□日本は人口密度の高い国です。

□日本は混み合った国です。

□日本は混み合った国です。とくに、東京、大阪に人が集中しています。

Size of Japan

The land area of Japan is approximately 378,000 square kilometers.

At 378,000 square kilometers, Japan is slightly larger than Germany.

Japan's land area is small compared with the United States, China, and Russia.

Japan is three-quarters the size of Spain.

Japan's National Strengths

Japan is the fourth-largest economy in the world.

Japan is a developed country.

Japan is a country with a highly developed infrastructure.

Japan is a country with a developed education system.

Safety in Japan

Japan is known for its low crime rate.

Japan is known for its low crime rate. According to statistics, the overall crime rate in Japan is about 15 percent of that in Canada.

Population of Japan

The population of Japan is approximately 120 million.

About 120 million people live in Japan.

Japan is a densely populated country.

Japan is a crowded country.

Japan is a crowded place. In particular, there are high concentrations of people in Tokyo and Osaka.

□ 日本の人口は1億2千万で、ニュージーランドのおよそ23倍です。

□ 日本の人口は1億2千万で、面積はスペインの4分の3です。

□ 日本は平地の少ない山がちな国で、そこに1億2千万の人が住んでいます。

日本の地勢

□ 日本は島国です。

□ 日本は島国で、6800以上の島があります。

□ 日本は主要4島からなる島国です。北から北海道、本州、四国、そして九州です。

□ 日本は島国で、6800以上の島があります。主な島は北から、北海道、本州、四国、九州です。

□ 日本は南北に長くのびた島国です。

□ 日本は島国で、数えきれないほどの湾や入り江があります。

□ 日本の海岸線は、たくさんの湾や入り江で複雑な地形をしています。

□ 最も大きな島は本州で、東京は本州にあります。

□ 本州は日本で一番大きな島で、イギリスより少し小さいです。

□ 日本は山がちな国です。

□ 日本は平地の少ない山がちな国です。

□ 日本には多くの火山があります。

Japan's population is 120 million, about 23 times the population of New Zealand.

Japan has a population of 120 million and is three-quarters the size of Spain.

Japan is a mountainous country with limited flatland, and 120 million people live there.

Geography of Japan

Japan is an island nation.

Japan is an island nation with more than 6,800 islands.

Japan is an island nation consisting of four main islands. From north to south, they are Hokkaido, Honshu, Shikoku, and Kyushu.

Japan is an island country with more than 6,800 islands. From the north, the main islands are Hokkaido, Honshu, Shikoku, and Kyushu.

Japan is an island nation that stretches a great distance from north to south.

Japan is an island nation with countless bays and inlets.

Japan's coastline is a complex terrain with many bays and inlets.

The largest island is Honshu, where Tokyo is located.

Honshu is the largest island in Japan, and its area is slightly smaller than that of the UK.

Japan is a mountainous country.

Japan is a mountainous country with little flatland.

Japan is an island country with many volcanoes.

□ 日本列島に山が多いのは、火山活動がとても活発な地域に位置しているからです。

□ 日本では多くの地震が起きます。

□ 日本列島には活火山が多いので、頻繁に地震が起きます。

□ 日本の平地は限られています。

□ 日本は山が多いので、平地はとても限られています。

□ 日本で一番大きな平野は、関東平野です。

□ 日本で一番大きな平野は、東京を囲む関東平野です。

□ 日本で一番大きな平野は関東平野で、ハワイ州とほぼ同じ面積です。

□ 東京を囲む日本で一番大きな平野は関東平野で、ハワイ州とほぼ同じ面積です。

The reason there are so many mountains in the Japanese archipelago is that it is located in a very active volcanic region.

Many earthquakes occur in Japan.

Because there are many active volcanoes in the Japanese archipelago, earthquakes occur frequently.

There is limited flatland in Japan.

Because of the mountainous nature of Japan, flatland is very limited.

The largest flat area in Japan is the Kanto Plain.

The largest flat area in Japan is the Kanto Plain, which surrounds Tokyo.

The largest plain in Japan is the Kanto Plain, which is about the same size as the State of Hawaii.

The largest flat area in Japan is the Kanto Plain, which surrounds Tokyo and is approximately the same size as the State of Hawaii.

日本の気候

☐ 日本のほぼ全域が温帯に属しています。

☐ 日本の気候は基本的には温暖です。

☐ 日本の気候は基本的には温暖ですが、北と南では大きく異なります。

☐ 日本は南北に長くのびているので、気候もさまざまです。

☐ 日本の春は快適です。

☐ 日本の春は温暖で快適です。

☐ 日本を訪れるなら春が最適です。

☐ 日本の雨季は梅雨といいます。

☐ 日本には梅雨とよばれる雨季があります。

☐ 日本には梅雨とよばれる雨季があり、その期間はじめじめしています。

☐ 日本の梅雨は6月から7月中旬までです。

☐ 梅雨とは雨季のことで、夏の前のその時期、暖かい気流と冷たい気流がぶつかり合います。

☐ 日本の夏は湿度が高いです。

☐ 日本の夏は暑いです。

☐ 日本の夏はじめじめとしています。

☐ 日本の夏は暑くて湿度が高いです。

Climate of Japan

Almost the entire area of Japan is in the temperate zone.

The climate of Japan is basically temperate.

The climate of Japan is basically temperate but varies from north to south.

Because Japan stretches a great distance from north to south, it has a variety of climates.

Japan has a comfortable spring.

Spring in Japan is warm and pleasant.

Spring is the best season to visit Japan.

The rainy season is called *tsuyu* in Japan.

Japan has a rainy season called *tsuyu*.

Japan has a rainy season called *tsuyu* and is humid in that period.

The rainy season in Japan lasts from June to mid-July.

The rainy season is the period before summer when warm and cold air currents collide.

Summers in Japan are humid.

Summers in Japan are hot.

Summer in Japan is humid.

Summer in Japan is hot and humid.

□ 日本の夏が暑くて湿度が高いのは、亜熱帯高気圧が暖かい気流を日本のほうに押し上げるからです。

□ 夏から秋の初めにかけて、台風と呼ばれる熱帯低気圧が日本にやってきます。

□ 日本のほかの地域に比べると、北海道は夏でも涼しいです。

□ 台風はハリケーンのようなもので、毎夏、太平洋から日本に向けてやってきます。

□ 秋は日本を旅するのにちょうどいい季節です。

□ 日本の秋の天候はとても快適です。

□ 晩秋になると北海道は寒くなります。

□ 10月下旬になると北海道には初雪が降ります。

□ 京都の紅葉は11月が見ごろです。

□ 九州の冬は比較的穏やかですが、北海道はとても寒いです。

樹氷

□ 本州の北西部では、冬になるとかなりの量の雪が降ります。

□ 日本の北部には、かなりの量の雪が降ります。

□ 日本の北部にはかなりの量の雪が降りますが、東部は冷たい風のため、寒くて乾燥しています。

□ 一般的には、日本を旅するなら天候もよい春と秋が最適です。

□ 日本では春になると、美しい桜を満喫することができます。

□ ヨーロッパや北米と同様、秋になると山や村では鮮やかな紅葉が楽しめます。

The Japanese summer is generally hot and humid because subtropical high pressure pushes warm air toward Japan.

From summer until the beginning of fall, Japan is hit by tropical storms called typhoons.

Compared with other parts of Japan, Hokkaido is cool in summer.

Typhoons are like hurricanes, and each summer, they come to Japan from the Pacific Ocean.

Autumn is a good time to travel in Japan.

Autumn weather in Japan is very pleasant.

In late fall, Hokkaido becomes colder.

In late October, Hokkaido receives its first snowfall.

November is the best time to see the autumn leaves in Kyoto.

Winters in Kyushu are relatively mild, but Hokkaido is very cold.

In the northwestern part of Honshu, a considerable amount of snow falls in winter.

A considerable amount of snow falls in the northern part of Japan.

While the northern part of Japan gets a large amount of snow, the eastern part is cold and dry due to the cold winds.

Generally speaking, spring and autumn are the best seasons to see Japan because of the weather.

In Japan, spring is the best time to enjoy the beautiful cherry blossoms.

As in Europe and North America, autumn brings brilliant autumn leaves in the mountains and villages.

日本語

□ 日本語がどこからきたのか、正確なことはわかっていません。

□ 韓国人やアジア北部の人々が似た言葉を話しています。

□ 日本語は、2千年にわたって小さな島々の中で、孤立してきました。

□ 中国の漢字は、5世紀から6世紀ごろに日本に伝わりました。

□ 中国の文字を日本では漢字といい、今日でも日本語を書くのに使われています。

□ 漢字は、日本語の文章に組み込まれて使われます。

□ 漢字は、日本語の文章に組み込まれて使われますが、中国語の文法の影響は受けません。

□ 日本語と中国語はまったく異なる言語です。

□ 日本語と中国語は異なる言語なので、中国語の文法に左右されずに漢字を使うことができます。

□ 日本語と中国語はまったく異なる言語ですが、書き文字として漢字を取り入れました。

□ 中国本土では簡略化された漢字が使われています。それらの文字は日本の漢字とは異なります。

□ 一つの漢字に対して、2種類の読み方があります。

□ 一つの漢字に対して、2種類の読み方があります。中国風の読み方を音読み、日本風に変更したものを訓読みといいます。

□ 漢字は日本で古くから使われてきたため、音読みも現在の中国語の発音とは異なります。

Japanese Language

It is not known exactly where the Japanese language came from.

Koreans and people of northern Asia speak similar languages.

The Japanese language has been isolated on a small group of islands for two millennia.

Chinese kanji were introduced to Japan around the 5th or 6th century.

The Chinese characters are called kanji in Japan and are still used today to write the Japanese language.

Kanji are used incorporated into Japanese writing.

Kanji characters are incorporated into Japanese sentences, but are not influenced by Chinese grammar.

Japanese and Chinese are completely different languages.

Because Japanese and Chinese are different languages, kanji can be used without being influenced by Chinese grammar.

Although Japanese is a completely different language from Chinese, Japan imported Chinese characters called kanji for use in the writing system.

In mainland China, people use simplified Chinese, and those characters are different from Japanese characters.

There are two ways of reading each Chinese character in Japan.

There are two ways of reading each Chinese character in Japan. The Chinese way is called the *onyomi* and the modified way is called the *kunyomi*.

Since Chinese characters have been used in Japan since ancient times, the *onyomi* reading differs from the current Chinese pronunciation.

□ 音読みは1700年以上にわたって日本語のなかで確立されてきたので、中国人も理解することはできません。

□ 漢字のほかに、日本人はカタカナとひらがなを使います。

□ 日本人はカタカナとひらがなという独自の表音文字を考案しました。

□ 9、10世紀ごろに、カタカナとひらがなは広まりました。

□ カタカナもひらがなも、漢字の表記から発達したものです。

□ ひらがなは日常の書き文字として使われています。

□ ひらがなは日常の書き文字に使われ、カタカナは外来語を表すときに使われます。

伊 → い
呂 → ろ
波 → は
仁 → に

□ 以前、カタカナは公式の書類などで使われていましたが、今では外来語を表すときに使われています。

□ 日本人は書くときに、漢字、カタカナ、ひらがなを一緒に使います。

□ 日本はその歴史を通して、外国語を受け入れ、（日本風に）変更してきました。

□ 昔は、数え切れないほどの言葉が、中国から輸入され、日本語に組み込まれていきました。

□ 輸入された言葉や表現は、外来語と呼ばれます。

□ 外来語は日本語の文法構造に組み込まれています。

□ 外来語はカタカナで表記され、日本式に発音します。

Since the *onyomi* have been evolving with the Japanese language for more than 1,700 years, Chinese people cannot understand them.

In addition to kanji, Japanese use katakana and hiragana.

The Japanese created their own phonetic writing systems called katakana and hiragana.

Katakana and hiragana came into common use around the 9th and 10th centuries.

Both katakana and hiragana were developed from Chinese characters.

Hiragana is used in everyday written characters.

Hiragana is used for everyday written characters, while katakana is used to represent foreign words.

Katakana used to be used for official documents, but now it is used to express foreign words.

Japanese people use kanji, katakana, and hiragana together when writing.

Throughout its history, Japan has accepted and changed foreign words (into a Japanese way).

In the past, countless words were imported from China and incorporated into the Japanese language.

Imported words and expressions are referred to as *gairaigo*.

Foreign words are incorporated into the grammatical structure of the Japanese language.

Foreign words are written in katakana and pronounced in the Japanese style.

＼ちょこっと／

知っておきたい日本紹介のコツ❶

ただ単に本書のフレーズを習得するだけではなく、少し意識するだけで外国人相手に伝わる日本紹介のコツと心構えをお伝えしていきます。

● 日本は素敵な国、でも特別な国ではないということ

外国の人に、日本の良いところを紹介するのは当然のことです。しかし、日本が他の国と違って特別な国であるという表現は慎みたいものです。例えば、世界中にはたくさんの島国があり、日本と同じように四季の変化を楽しめる国もたくさんあります。日本を特別扱いするような言い回しは、逆に相手に不快感や懸念を抱かせてしまいます。

× **We have four beautiful seasons in Japan.**
日本には美しい四季があります。

○ **Japan has four distinctive seasons, as you may have in your country.**
日本は四季の変化が際立っています。あなたの国もそうかもしれませんが。

● あまりおすすめではない表現

日本を紹介するとき、「We Japanese ～（我々日本人は～）」と表現してしまうことがあります。しかし、これは相手と日本人である自分たちを区別して扱う印象を与えてしまいます。ここではあえて客観性を持たせ The Japanese ～ とする、あるいは他の表現を考えてみましょう。

× **We Japanese don't have such a custom.**
我々日本人にはそうした習慣はありません。

○ **I don't think there is a custom like that in Japan.**

また、相手に何かすることを提案するときに「You had better ～（～すべきです）」という表現を使っているかもしれませんが、これは相手に強制するような強い表現なので、あまりおすすめできません。

× **You had better visit Kyoto.**
京都に行くべきです。

○ **I recommend that you visit Kyoto.**

● とはいえカジュアルに

何をおいても堅苦しくならず、多少の文法や発音のミスは気にせず、笑顔で相手と接しましょう。世界中で話されている英語には各々の発音や言い回しがあり、日本人が話す英語に日本人独特の癖があっても、それは案外受け入れられるものです。完璧にこだわって堅苦しくなるよりも、多少くだけていても楽しく付き合える方が相手からの印象も良いでしょう。場数を踏めば、だんだんとあなたの英語は上達するはずです。

第❷章

日本を楽しむ

日本の世界遺産
日本の魅力
日本の今を楽しむ
日本食を楽しむ

世界遺産マップ

日本の世界遺産は25ヵ所で、そのうち5ヵ所（屋久島、白神山地、知床、小笠原諸島、奄美・沖縄）が、自然遺産に登録されています。

奈良
法隆寺地域の仏教建造物
☞ Horyuji Temple p.37
京都・滋賀
古都京都の文化財
☞ Ancient Capital of Kyoto p.37
兵庫
姫路城
☞ Himeji Castle p.39
島根
石見銀山遺跡とその文化的景観
☞ Iwami Ginzan Silver Mine p.39
福岡
「神宿る島」宗像・沖ノ島と関連遺産群
☞ Munakata/Okinoshima Island and Related Heritage Sites p.43
広島
厳島神社
☞ Itsukushima Jinja p.39
広島
原爆ドーム
☞ Hiroshima Peace Memorial Park p.39
大阪
百舌鳥・古市古墳群
☞ Mozu and Furuichi Tumulus Group p.45
奈良
古都奈良の文化財
☞ Ancient Capital o
p.37
鹿児島
屋久島
☞ Yakushima Island p.39
長崎・熊本
長崎と天草地方の潜伏キリシタン関連遺産群
☞ "Hidden Christian Sites" in Nagasaki and the Amakusa Region p.43
和歌山・奈良・三重
紀伊山地の霊場と参詣道
☞ Kumano Kodo p.37
沖縄
琉球王国のグスク及び関連遺産群
☞ Gusuku of the Ryukyu Kingdom p.41
鹿児島・沖縄
奄美大島、徳之島、沖縄北部及び西表島
☞ Amami/Okinawa p.45

福岡・佐賀・長崎・熊本・鹿児島・山口・岩手・静岡
明治日本の産業革命遺産—製鉄・製鋼，造船，石炭産業
☞ Industrial Revolution Heritage of Meiji Japan *p.43*

日本の世界遺産

日本の世界遺産の登録数は、25件で世界11位です。日本が世界に誇る各遺産の特徴を、英語で紹介してみましょう。

概要

□ 日本にはユネスコの世界遺産が25ヵ所あります。自然遺産が5ヵ所で、文化遺産が20ヵ所です。

知床

□ 知床半島は北海道の北東部に位置し、素晴らしい自然と野生生物を見ることができます。

□ 知床半島はその美しい自然と野生生物が認められ、世界遺産に認定されています。

白神山地

□ 青森と秋田の境に白神山地はあり、野生ブナ林と山々が世界遺産に認定されています。

□ 白神山地は、貴重なブナ林で覆われた山々で、ユネスコの世界遺産に認定されています。

日光の社寺

□ 日光には山、湖、有名な社寺があり、よく知られた国立公園で世界遺産にも指定されています。

□ 日光国立公園は有名な寺社のほか、山、湖などの豊かな景観に恵まれており、世界遺産に指定されています。

□ 日光は栃木県にあり、徳川幕府の初代将軍である徳川家康を祀る東照宮のほかに、その自然の豊さでも有名です。

Track 03

Overview

There are 25 UNESCO World Heritage Sites in Japan. Five are natural heritage sites and 20 are cultural heritage sites.

Shiretoko

The Shiretoko Peninsula is located in the northeastern part of Hokkaido, and you can see wonderful nature and wildlife there.

The Shiretoko Peninsula has been designated a World Heritage Site in recognition of its beautiful nature and wildlife.

Shirakami Sanchi

The Shirakami Sanchi is located on the border of Aomori and Akita, and its wild beech forests and mountains have been recognized as a World Heritage Site.

The Shirakami Sanchi is designated as a UNESCO World Heritage Site for mountains covered by precious wild-beech forests.

Shrines and Temples of Nikko

Nikko, with its mountains, lakes, and famous temples and shrines, is a well-known national park, and is also designated as a World Heritage Site.

Nikko National Park is blessed with famous temples and shrines, as well as mountains, lakes, and other rich landscapes, and is designated as a World Heritage Site.

Nikko is located in Tochigi Prefecture and is famous for its abundant nature as well as for Toshogu Shrine, which is dedicated to Tokugawa Ieyasu, the first shogun of the Tokugawa Shogunate.

白川郷と五箇山

□ 白川郷と五箇山は、伝統的な急勾配の茅葺き屋根の家が保存されていることから、世界遺産に指定されています。

□ 白川郷や五箇山周辺には、急勾配の茅葺き屋根の集落が点在しています。

熊野古道

□ 紀伊半島にある熊野古道は、古くからの巡礼の道で、ユネスコ世界遺産に登録されています。

□ 熊野古道は、紀伊半島の深い森や谷に点在する隠れた寺社と伊勢神宮を結んでいます。

古都京都

□ 寺、神社、古民家、そして昔ながらの雰囲気が残る京都は、世界でも最も有名な世界遺産です。

□ 京都はかつての日本の首都というだけではありません。伝統工芸や儀式の中心地でもあるのです。

古都奈良

□ 奈良とその周辺には古代からの寺が残っており、ユネスコの世界遺産に登録されています。

□ 奈良は、古代シルクロードの終点であることから、世界遺産に登録されています。

□ 奈良周辺には、インド、中国、さらには古代西洋人の影響を受けて1000年以上前にできた村が点在しています。

法隆寺

□ 法隆寺周辺は、ユネスコの世界遺産に登録されています。法隆寺が大陸の影響を受けた世界最古の木造建築だからです。

□ 法隆寺とその周辺を斑鳩（いかるが）と呼び、ここは7世紀初頭、聖徳太子が日本を治めた地でもあります。

Shirakawa-go and Gokayama

The historic villages of Shirakawa-go and Gokayama are designated as World Heritage Sites for their traditional houses with steep thatched roofs.

The villages around Shirakawa-go and Gokayama are dotted with houses that have steep thatched-roofs.

Kumano Kodo

The Kumano Kodo, located on the Kii Peninsula, is an ancient pilgrimage route and a UNESCO World Heritage Site.

The Kumano Kodo connects the Ise-Jingu Shrine with hidden temples and shrines scattered in the deep forests and valleys of the Kii Peninsula.

Ancient Capital of Kyoto

Kyoto, with its temples, shrines, old houses, and old-fashioned atmosphere, is one of the most famous World Heritage Sites in the world.

Kyoto is not just the ancient capital of Japan. It is also the center of traditional craftmanship and ceremonies.

Ancient Capital of Nara

Ancient temples remain in and around Nara, which is registered as a UNESCO World Heritage Site.

Nara is on the World Heritage List because it is the terminus of the ancient Silk Road.

In the Nara area, you will see countless villages built more than a thousand years ago and influenced by Indian and Chinese people, and even ancient Westerners.

Horyuji Temple

Horyuji Temple and its vicinity is designated as a UNESCO World Heritage Site because Horyuji is the oldest wooden structure in the world and shows the influence of continental Asia.

Horyuji Temple and its vicinity is called Ikaruga, and this is also where Prince Shotoku ruled Japan in the early 7th century.

姫路城

□ 姫路城はその美しいたたずまいで知られ、世界遺産となっています。

□ 現存する大天守は17世紀に建築されたもので、その美しさと優雅な姿から、白鷺城（しらさぎじょう）とも呼ばれます。

広島平和記念公園

□ 平和記念公園は、原爆が落とされた広島の中心部にあり、世界遺産になっています。

□ 平和記念公園には、原爆ドームとよばれる原爆被害を受けた建物と、原爆資料を展示したミュージアムがあります。

石見銀山

□ 石見（いわみ）銀山とその周辺は、2007年に世界遺産に登録されました。

□ 石見銀山は、開発された16世紀当時、世界最大の銀山でした。鉱山だけでなく、周囲の町や建物などもよく保存されています。

厳島神社

□ 12世紀にできた厳島神社は、神道で神聖な場所とされる宮島の海辺に建立されました。

□ 広島の西に位置する厳島神社は、1996年に世界遺産に登録されました。

屋久島

□ 屋久島は、鹿児島県沖の南西諸島の一部です。自生のスギや険しい山などが、1993年に世界遺産に登録されました。

□ 屋久島は、貴重な森林、野生生物、山などあらゆるものが小さな島に集中しているという点で、他にはない場所です。

Himeji Castle

Himeji Castle is known for its beauty and is designated as a World Heritage Site.

The existing main keep was built in the 17th century and is also called Shirasagijo Castle, or White Egret Castle, because of its beauty and elegance.

Hiroshima Peace Memorial Park

Peace Memorial Park, located in the center of Hiroshima, where the atomic bomb was dropped, is a World Heritage Site.

The Peace Memorial Park includes the Atomic Bomb Dome, a building damaged by the bomb, and a museum exhibiting items related to the atomic bomb.

Iwami Ginzan Silver Mine

Iwami Ginzan Silver Mine and its vicinity was designated as a World Heritage Site in 2007.

Iwami Ginzan was the world's largest silver mine when it was developed in the 16th century. Not only the mine, but also the surrounding towns and buildings have been well preserved.

Itsukushima Jinja

Itsukushima Shrine, established in the 12th century, was built on the seashore of Miyajima, a place considered sacred in Shintoism.

Itsukushima Shrine, located west of Hiroshima, was designated as a World Heritage Site in 1996.

Yakushima Island

Yakushima is part of the Nansei Islands off the coast of Kagoshima Prefecture. Its native cedars and rugged mountains were designated as a World Heritage Site in 1993.

Yakushima is unique in that everything from precious forests, wildlife, and mountains is concentrated on a small island.

琉球王国のグスク

□ グスクとは沖縄の島々に点在する琉球王国時代の城や遺跡で、中国の影響が見られる見事な建築物です。2000年に世界遺産となりました。

□ 復元された首里城では、かつての独立王朝時代の雰囲気を味わうことができましたが、2019年の火災によって焼失してしまいました。

平泉

□ 平泉とその周辺地域は、古代の仏教寺院によって2011年に世界遺産に登録されました。

□ 平泉は岩手県に位置しています。この町は、平安時代末期、東北地方の中心地として栄えました。中尊寺は9世紀に建てられ、今でも当時の荘厳さを残しています。

小笠原諸島

□ 小笠原諸島は東京の南、約1000kmに点在します。小笠原諸島は独自の自然が残り、太平洋と日本の文化が混在することで知られています。2011年に世界遺産に登録されました。

□ 小笠原諸島は、東京のはるか南の太平洋上に位置しています。その中の一つ、硫黄島は、太平洋戦争の時、激しい戦場となったことで知られています。

富士山

□ 富士山は、日本で17番目の世界遺産です。

□ 富士山は自然だけでなく、信仰や芸術を生み出した山としても価値が認められました。

Gusuku of the Ryukyu Kingdom

Gusuku are castles and ruins from the Ryukyu Kingdom period scattered throughout the islands of Okinawa, stunning architectural structures with Chinese influences that became a World Heritage Site in 2000.

The restored Shuri Castle provided a taste of the atmosphere of the once independent dynasty, but was destroyed by fire in 2019.

Hiraizumi

Hiraizumi and its surrounding area was designated as a World Heritage Site in 2011 due to its ancient Buddhist temples.

Hiraizumi is located in Iwate Prefecture. The town flourished as the center of the Tohoku region in the late Heian period (794-1185). Chuson-ji Temple was built in the 9th century and still retains the grandeur of its time.

Ogasawara Islands

The Ogasawara Islands are located about 1,000 km south of Tokyo. They are known for their unique natural environment and the blend of Pacific and Japanese cultures. They were registered as a World Heritage Site in 2011.

The Ogasawara Islands are located in the Pacific Ocean, far south of Tokyo. One of the islands, Iwo Jima, is known for the terrible battle fought there during World War II.

Mt. Fuji

Mt. Fuji is Japan's 17th World Heritage Site.

Mt. Fuji was recognized not only for its natural beauty, but also for its value as a mountain that gave birth to faith and art.

富岡製糸場

□ 富岡製糸場は、日本初の本格的な機械製糸の工場です。

□ 富岡製糸場は、1872年の開業当時の様子がよく保存されています。

明治日本の産業革命遺産

□ 幕末から明治にかけて日本が急速な産業化を成し遂げたことを示す遺産群です。遺産は8つの県に点在しています。

□ 製鉄・製鋼業、造船業、石炭産業は日本の基幹産業です。

ル・コルビュジエの建築作品

□ ル・コルビュジエはパリを拠点に活躍した建築家です。日本からは国立西洋美術館の建築が世界遺産に登録されました。

□ 国立西洋美術館は東京の上野公園にあり、西洋美術を専門とする日本で唯一の国立美術館です。

宗像・沖ノ島と関連遺産

□ 福岡県にある沖ノ島や関連する史跡群は、自然崇拝を現代まで継承している点が評価されて、世界遺産になりました。

□ 沖ノ島は、島そのものが神として崇拝されているため、特別な許可がない限り上陸することはできません。

長崎と天草地方の「潜伏キリシタン」関連遺産

□ 長崎県と熊本県の天草地方には「潜伏キリシタン」の遺産が多く残っています。

□「潜伏キリシタン」とは、かつて禁止されていたキリスト教の信仰を密かに守り続けた人々のことです。

Tomioka Silk Mill

Tomioka Silk Mill was Japan's first full-scale mechanical silk mill.

The Tomioka Silk Mill has been well-preserved so as to retain its original appearance from when it opened in 1872.

Industrial Revolution Heritage of Meiji Japan

This group of heritage sites demonstrates the rapid industrialization of Japan from the end of the Edo period to the Meiji era. The heritage sites are scattered across eight prefectures.

Iron and steel manufacturing, shipbuilding, and the coal industry are key industries in Japan.

Le Corbusier's Architectural Works

Le Corbusier was an architect based in Paris. In Japan, the architecture of the National Museum of Western Art was registered as a World Heritage Site.

The National Museum of Western Art, located in Ueno Park in Tokyo, is the only national museum in Japan dedicated to Western art.

Munakata/Okinoshima Island and Related Heritage Sites

Okinoshima Island and a group of related historic sites in Fukuoka Prefecture were designated World Heritage Sites in recognition of the fact that they have carried on the worship of nature to the present day.

Because the island itself is worshipped as a god, no one is allowed to land on Okinoshima without special permission.

"Hidden Christian Sites" in Nagasaki and the Amakusa Region

Many "hidden Christian sites" remain in Nagasaki and the Amakusa Region of Kumamoto Prefecture.

The term "Hidden Christians" refers to those who secretly continued to follow the Christian faith, which was once forbidden.

百舌鳥・古市古墳群

□ 大阪府にある大小さまざまな形をした49基の古墳は、2019年に世界遺産に登録されました。

□ 古墳とは、日本の古代につくられたお墓のことで、埋葬された人の身分によってその大きさや形が異なります。

奄美・沖縄

□ 鹿児島県の奄美大島と徳之島、沖縄県の沖縄本島の北部と西表島の４島が世界遺産に登録されました。

□ 多様な生物の生息地として評価された４つの島には、絶滅危惧種に指定されている生物もいます。

北海道・北東北の縄文遺跡群

□ 北海道、青森、岩手、秋田にある縄文時代の遺跡群が2021年に世界遺産に登録されました。

□ これらの遺跡は縄文時代の集落で、狩りや漁、植物の採集によって定住していた当時の人々の生活と精神文化を示しています。

青森県の三内丸山遺跡

Mozu and Furuichi Tumulus Group

Forty-nine *kofun* tumuli of various sizes and shapes in Osaka Prefecture were registered as a World Heritage Site in 2019.

Kofun tumuli are tombs created in ancient Japan and vary in size and shape according to the status of the person buried in them.

Amami/Okinawa

Four islands, including Amami Oshima and Tokunoshima in Kagoshima Prefecture, and the northern part of Okinawa's main island and Iriomotejima in Okinawa Prefecture, were registered as World Heritage Sites.

The four islands were recognized as habitats for a diversity of living creatures, some of which are listed as endangered species.

Jomon Sites in Hokkaido and Northern Tohoku

Jomon Period sites in Hokkaido, Aomori, Iwate, and Akita were registered as World Heritage Sites in 2021.

These sites are Jomon-era settlements that illustrate the lifestyle and spiritual culture of the people of the time, who settled there by hunting, fishing, and gathering plants.

日本の温泉と旅館

Japanese *Onsen* and *Ryokan*

主な温泉地

❶	登別	Noboribetsu
❷	酸ケ湯	Sukayu
❸	花巻	Hanamaki
❹	蔵王	Zao
❺	秋保	Akiu
❻	飯坂	Iizaka
❼	鬼怒川	Kinugawa
❽	四万	Shima
❾	伊香保	Ikaho
❿	草津	Kusatsu
⓫	箱根	Hakone
⓬	熱海・湯河原	Atami, Yugawara
⓭	修善寺	Shuzenji
⓮	別所	Bessho
⓯	奥飛騨	Okuhida
⓰	和倉	Wakura
⓱	下呂	Gero
⓲	城崎	Kinosaki
⓳	有馬	Arima
⓴	湯の峰	Yunomine
㉑	道後	Dogo
㉒	別府・湯布院	Beppu, Yufuin
㉓	黒川	Kurokawa
㉔	指宿	Ibusuki

(☞ *Onsen, p.51*)

Bath 風呂

Large public bath 大浴場

Ryokan, traditional Japanese inn （☞ *Ryokan p.53*）
旅館

Ryokan staff
旅館のスタッフ

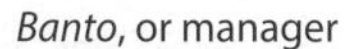

Banto, or manager
番頭

Ryorinin, chef
料理人

Okami, or female manager
女将

Nakai gashira, housekeeper
仲居頭

Nakai, maid
仲居

Rooms
部屋

Meals
食事

Dinner
夕食

日本の家屋

(☞Japanese Houses *p.55*)

Traditional Japanese House

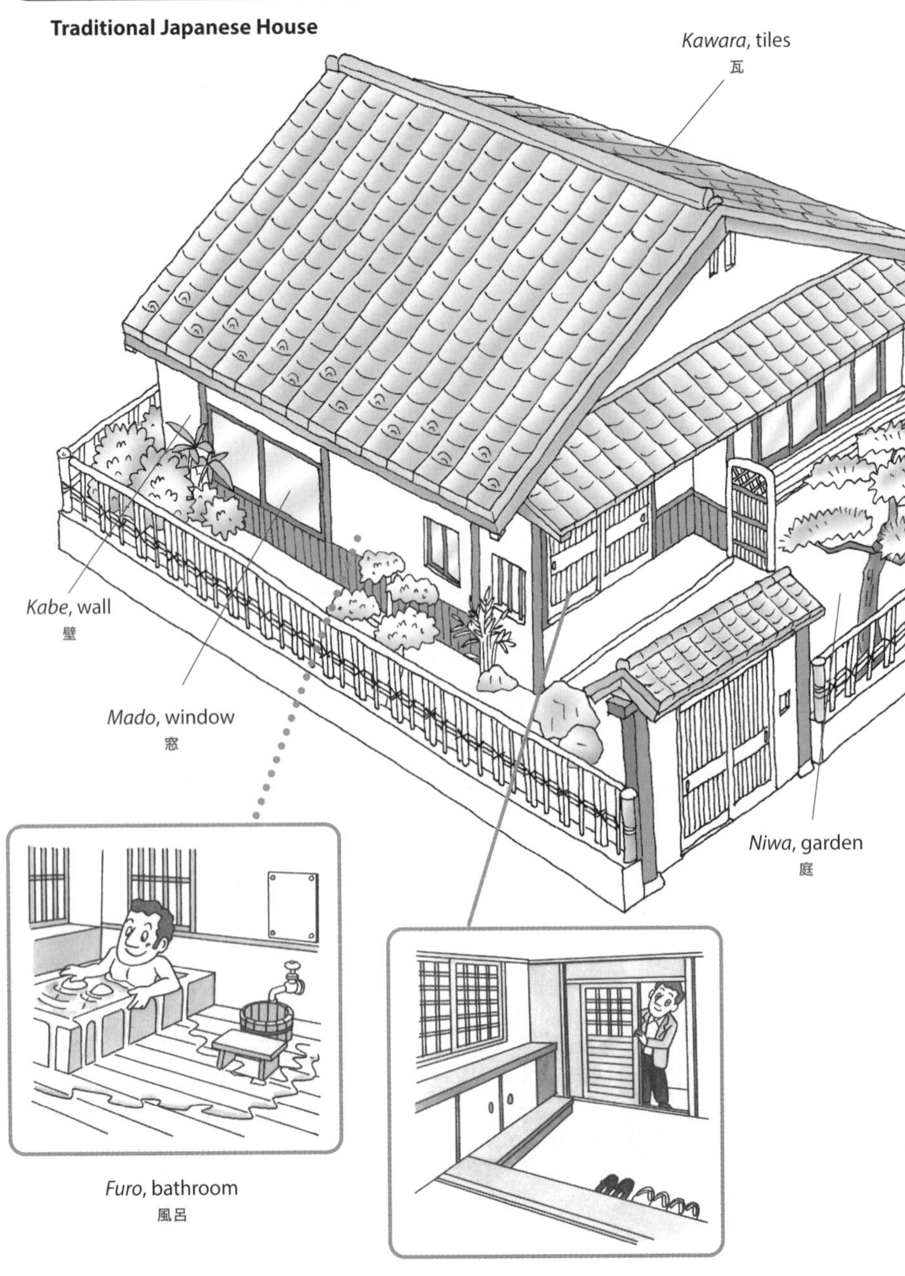

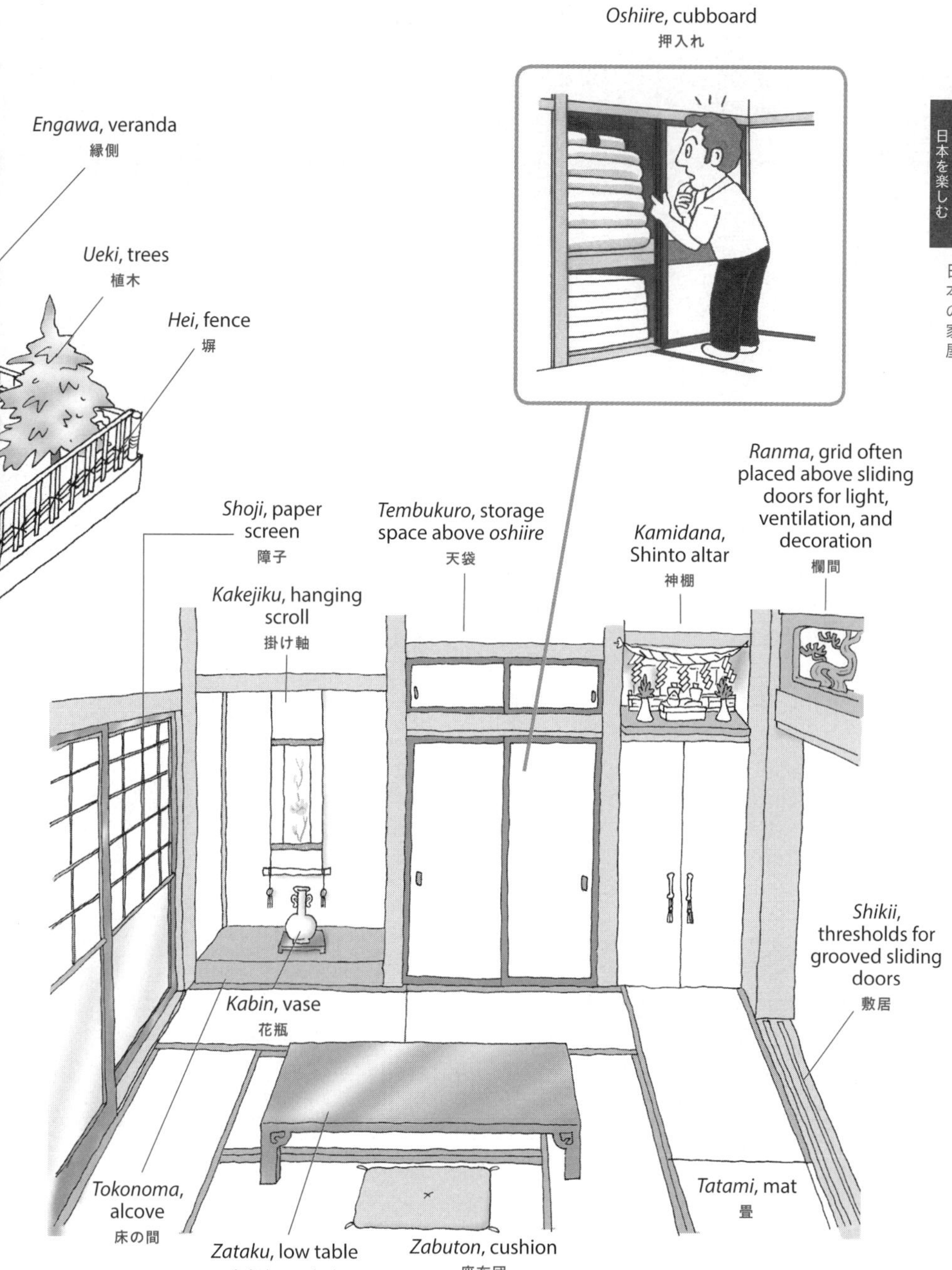
Oshiire, cubboard
押入れ
Engawa, veranda
縁側
Ueki, trees
植木
Hei, fence
塀
Shoji, paper screen
障子
Tembukuro, storage space above *oshiire*
天袋
Kamidana, Shinto altar
神棚
Ranma, grid often placed above sliding doors for light, ventilation, and decoration
欄間
Kakejiku, hanging scroll
掛け軸
Kabin, vase
花瓶
Shikii, thresholds for grooved sliding doors
敷居
Tokonoma, alcove
床の間
Tatami, mat
畳
Zataku, low table
座卓（テーブル）
Zabuton, cushion
座布団

日本の魅力

日本では全国至るところに温泉があります。温泉宿は、部屋、食事、庭など、日本らしさが満載です。

温泉

□ 日本人は温泉が大好きです。

□ 日本は火山列島なので、至るところに温泉があります。

□ 日本人は、全国各地にある温泉を楽しみます。

□ 温泉は日本の至るところにあります。

□ 温泉は日本の至るところにあります。温泉は山間の渓谷だけでなく、海岸沿いにもあります。

□ 温泉保養地を訪れると、日本の都市部にはない落ち着いた地域色を感じるでしょう。

□ 温泉は健康維持のために日本人に楽しまれています。というのも、温泉には地域によって様々な種類のミネラルが含まれているからです。

□ 多くの場合、旅館に泊まって温泉を楽しみます。

□ 温泉は旅館の中にもあります。すなわち、旅館で温泉に入浴できるのです。

□ 体を癒すために長期にわたって温泉地に滞在する人もいます。

□ 湯治とは、病気を治すために長期間温泉地に滞在することです。

南紀勝浦の温泉風景

Track 04

湯布院の露天風呂

Onsen (Hot Springs)

Japanese people love hot springs.

Since Japan is a volcanic archipelago, there are hot springs everywhere.

Japanese people enjoy hot springs located throughout the country.

Hot springs are found everywhere in Japan.

Hot springs are everywhere in Japan. They can be found along the coast as well as in mountain valleys.

When you visit a hot spring resort, you will experience a relaxed local atmosphere that you will not find in urban areas of Japan.

Hot springs are enjoyed by the Japanese for maintaining good health. This is because hot springs contain various types of minerals, depending on the region.

In many cases, people stay at *ryokan*, or Japanese inns, to enjoy hot springs.

Hot springs can also be found in *ryokan*. In other words, you can bathe in hot springs at *ryokan*.

Some people stay at hot springs for a long period of time to heal their bodies.

Toji means to stay at a hot spring for a long time to heal oneself from an illness.

□東京のような都市では、銭湯という公衆浴場があります。

旅館

□旅館は伝統的な日本の宿泊所です。

□旅館では伝統的な和室でくつろぐことができます。

□多くの旅館では、夕食と朝食は（宿泊費に）含まれています。

□一般的に、旅館では伝統的な日本食が振る舞われます。

□旅館の中には、伝統的な和風建築で建てられたものや、日本庭園があるものもあります。

□多くの旅館には温泉があります。

□午後、旅館にチェックインしたら、温泉に入ったり散策してから、酒やビールで夕食を楽しむことができます。

□ほとんどの場合、旅館では伝統的な日本の寝具である布団で寝ます。

□布団は旅館の従業員が部屋に敷きます。

□夕食を終えてから温泉や散策を楽しむこともできます。部屋を出ている間に、布団を敷いてくれます。

□ほとんどの旅館では、朝食前に布団を片付けます。

□旅館のチェックアウト時間は概して、普通のホテルよりも早いです。

□主要都市の観光地には、英語の通じる旅館がいくつかあります。

□「素泊まり」とは、食事をつけずに旅館に泊まることです。

In cities like Tokyo, there are public baths called *sento*.

Ryokan (Traditional Japanese Inns)

Ryokan are traditional Japanese inns.

At a *ryokan*, you can relax in a traditional Japanese-style room.

At many *ryokan*, dinner and breakfast are included.

Typically, *ryokans* serve traditional Japanese food.

Some *ryokan* have traditional Japanese buildings and gardens.

Many *ryokan* have hot spring baths.

After checking into a *ryokan* in the afternoon, you can enjoy the hot spring or take a stroll before enjoying dinner with sake or beer.

In most cases, people sleep on futons, or traditional Japanese sleeping mats, in *ryokan*.

The futon is laid out in your room by *ryokan* employees.

After you finish dinner, you can enjoy an *onsen* again or take a stroll, and while you are out, your futon will be set out.

In most *ryokan*, your futon is put away before breakfast.

Checkout time at *ryokan* is generally earlier than at ordinary hotels.

There are some English-speaking *ryokan* in major tourist areas.

Sudomari means to stay at a *ryokan* without having meal service.

日本家屋

□ 伝統的な日本家屋は木造です。

□ 伝統的な日本家屋は、あらゆる箇所を熟練した大工が施工します。

□ 伝統的な家屋を維持するのはとても費用がかかります。

□ もし日本で本格的な日本式の家屋を体験したければ、寺を訪れるか旅館という宿泊施設を利用してください。

□ 京都には町屋という伝統的な日本の商家が多くあります。

畳

□ 伝統的な日本間の床は畳が敷かれています。

□ 畳は柔らかいイ草を織ってつくられます。

□ 畳は日本独特のもので、和室の床材として使われる敷物の一種です。表面は、柔らかいイ草で覆われています。

□ 畳は暑くて湿気の多い夏に適しています。というのも、織ったイ草は通気がよく、肌触りが涼しいからです。

□ 畳は家の底部を断熱し保温するので、冬にも適しています。

瓦

□ 伝統的な日本家屋の屋根は瓦で覆われています。

□ 瓦は寺院建築に伴って、中国から伝来しました。

□ 古い日本家屋は古民家と呼ばれ、非常に数が少なく貴重なものです。

Japanese Houses

Traditional Japanese houses are made of wood.

Every part of a traditional Japanese house is constructed by skilled carpenters.

Maintaining such traditional houses can be very expensive.

If you would like to experience an authentic traditional house in Japan, visit a temple or an inn called a *ryokan*.

In Kyoto, there are many traditional Japanese merchant houses called *machiya*.

Tatami mats

The floors of traditional Japanese rooms are covered with *tatami* mats.

Tatami is made of woven soft rushes.

Tatami mats are unique to Japan and are a type of mat used as flooring material in Japanese-style rooms. The surface is covered with soft rushes.

Tatami is suitable for hot and humid summers. This is because woven rushes are breathable and cool to the touch.

Tatami is also suitable for winter because of its excellent heat retention properties at the bottom of the house.

Kawara (Tiles)

The roofs of traditional Japanese houses are covered with tiles known as *kawara*.

Tiles were introduced from China as part of the construction of temples.

Old Japanese houses are called *kominka*, and they are quite rare and precious.

襖

□ 伝統的な日本間には襖というスライド式のドアがあります。

□ 襖は和紙という伝統的な日本の紙で覆われています。

押し入れ

□ 多くの和室には押し入れという収納スペースがあり、襖で仕切られています。

□ 押し入れとは、寝具などを入れる収納スペースのことで、襖で仕切られています。

障子

□ 障子は伝統的な日本家屋で使われ、部屋と廊下を仕切るものです。

□ 障子とは、木の枠に薄くて白い和紙を貼ったスライド式のドアのことです。

床の間

□ 床の間とは客間にある壁に埋め込まれたスペースのことで、趣のある品々が飾られています。

□ 床の間とは客間の壁に特別に設えられた小さなスペースのことで、掛け軸の前に生け花を飾ったりします。

□ 床の間とは茶道が行われる部屋にある小さなスペースのことです。

Fusuma (Sliding Doors)

Traditional Japanese-style rooms have sliding doors called *fusuma*.

Fusuma sliding doors are covered with *washi*, a traditional Japanese paper.

Oshiire (Closet)

Many traditional Japanese rooms have storage spaces called *oshiire*, and they are separated by sliding doors.

An *oshiire* is a storage space for bedding and other items, and is partitioned off by sliding doors.

Shoji (Sliding Paper Doors)

Shoji sliding paper doors are used in traditional Japanese houses to separate rooms and hallways.

A *shoji* is a sliding door with a wooden frame covered with thin, white Japanese paper.

Tokonoma (Alcoves)

A *tokonoma* is a recessed space in a Japanese-style guest room, in which items for artistic appreciation are displayed.

An alcove is a small space specially set up on the wall of a guest room where ikebana arrangements are displayed in front of hanging scrolls.

An alcove is a small space in a room where the tea ceremony is held.

茶の間

神棚

□ 茶の間とは家族が集まる部屋です。

□ 茶の間には小さな神社を模した神棚が祀られていることがあります。

□ 囲炉裏のある茶の間もあります。その炉は調理にも使われます。

□ 囲炉裏とは和室に設えられた炉で、木や炭を燃やして暖をとったり、調理するのに使います。

仏間・仏壇

日本の家庭の典型的な仏壇

□ 仏間とは仏教のしきたりに則って祖先に手を合わせる部屋のことです。

□ 多くの伝統的な家には仏間があり、そこには仏壇が置かれています。

□ 仏壇とは、伝統的な祭壇のことで、祖先の魂が祀られます。

今の日本家屋

□ 現代の日本家屋の伝統的な日本間は和室と呼ばれます。

□ 現代の日本家屋の伝統的な日本間は和室と呼ばれ、西洋式の部屋は洋室と呼ばれます。

□ 現代の日本の家は、ほとんどが洋室で、伝統的な和室が1 ～ 2部屋あります。

Chanoma (Tea Room)

A *chanoma* is a room where the family gathers.

A *chanoma* may have a Shinto altar modeled after a small shrine.

Some *chanoma* have an *irori*, or open hearth. The hearth is also used for cooking.

An *irori* is an open hearth set in a traditional Japanese room to burn wood or charcoal for heat or cooking.

Butsuma (Prayer Room) and *Butsudan* (Buddhist Altar)

A *butsuma* is a room in which people pay homage to their ancestors in accordance with Buddhist custom.

Many traditional houses have a prayer room, where a Buddhist altar is placed.

A *butsudan* is a traditional altar where the souls of ancestors are worshipped.

Japanese Houses of Today

Traditionally styled Japanese rooms in modern Japanese houses are called *washitsu*.

The traditional Japanese-style room in a modern Japanese house is called a *washitsu*, while a Western-style room is called a *yoshitsu*.

Most modern Japanese houses are Western-style rooms with one or two traditional Japanese-style rooms.

日本庭園

□ 日本風の庭は日本庭園と呼ばれます。

□ 日本の多くの寺、旅館、伝統的な家屋には日本庭園があります。

□ 多くの日本庭園には池泉(ちせん)という池があります。

□ 苔と木で覆われた岩や池を配置することは、日本庭園の重要な要素です。

□ 魅力的な日本庭園をつくるためには、形のいい岩や木が必要です。

□ 錦鯉とは大切に育てられた鯉で、色が美しいことで知られています。

□ 錦鯉は伝統的な日本庭園の池によくいます。

□ 枯山水とは、池のない伝統的な日本庭園のことです。

□ 枯山水は水を用いず、砂、石、苔を使って、山や川、海などの自然景観を表現します。

□ 石庭は、主に石だけで作る庭のことで、枯山水を最小限にした庭と言えます。

□ 坪庭とは日本家屋にある小さな中庭のことです。

□ 坪庭は京都の商家である町屋によく見られる小さな中庭です。

日本三大名園のひとつ、後楽園（岡山市）

Japanese Gardens

Japanese gardens are called *Nihon teien.*

Many temples, *ryokan*, and traditional houses in Japan have Japanese gardens.

Many Japanese gardens have a pond called a *chisen*.

The placement of rocks and ponds covered with moss and trees is an important element of Japanese gardening.

Beautifully shaped rocks and trees are necessary to create an attractive Japanese garden.

Nishikigoi are carefully cultivated carp, known for their beautiful colors.

Nishikigoi are often found in ponds in traditional Japanese gardens.

A *karesansui* is a traditional Japanese garden without a pond.

Instead of water, *karesansui* use sand, stones, and moss to depict natural scenery, such as mountains, rivers, and the sea.

A *sekitei*, or stone garden, is a garden made mainly of stones and can be described as a minimalist version of a *karesansu*i.

A *tsuboniwa* is a small courtyard garden in a Japanese house.

A *tsuboniwa* is a small courtyard often found in *machiya*, the merchant houses of Kyoto.

日本の今を楽しむ

あらゆる家電が安価で入手できる日本の量販店は、訪日外国人にも人気のスポットです。伝統品から食品・日常用品がそろう百貨店も勧めてみましょう。

量販店

□ 大都市では量販店という大型店で買い物を楽しむことができます。

□ 家電量販店では、電気製品だけでなく、日用品、薬、食品などあらゆる商品を販売します。

□ 東京では、主要駅の周辺に家電を扱う量販店があります。

□ 特に、東京の秋葉原には、家電を扱う量販店が多くあります。

□ 量販店には、ビックカメラ、ヤマダ電機、ベスト電器、ヨドバシカメラ、ソフマップなどがあります。

□ 大都市には、文具や目新しい商品を扱う量販店があります。

□ ハンズやロフトといった大型店では、外国人に人気の文房具やオリジナル商品を売っています。

百貨店

□ 百貨店では、伝統的な和物から日常生活用品まで、あらゆるものを扱っています。

□ 日本の百貨店の地下は食品売り場になっており、特産品なども多く売っています。

□ 日本の百貨店の食品売り場に行くと、特産品の他、日本酒などのアルコール飲料も売っています。

日本橋の老舗デパート

Track 05

秋葉原

Ryohanten (Mega Stores)

In large cities, you can enjoy shopping at large stores called *ryohanten*.

In addition to electrical products, *kaden-ryohanten* sell all kinds of products, including daily necessities, medicines, and food products.

In Tokyo, mega stores selling home electronics can be found around major train stations.

In particular, Akihabara in Tokyo has many mega stores that sell home electronics.

Mega stores include Bic Camera, Yamada Denki, Best Denki, Yodobashi Camera, and Sofmap.

Large cities have mega stores that sell stationery and novelty items.

Mega stores such as Hands and Loft sell stationery and original products popular among foreigners.

Department Stores

Department stores sell everything from traditional Japanese goods to everyday household items.

The basement floor of a Japanese department store is for food products, and you can find many local delicacies there.

In addition to local specialties, alcoholic beverages, such as sake, are also sold in the food section of Japanese department stores.

新幹線・鉄道

□ 列車で日本を旅するのは楽しいものです。

□ 新幹線とは日本の高速列車の名前です。

□ 日本のほとんどの主要都市には新幹線という高速列車で行くことができます。

□ 新幹線はその姿形からよく弾丸列車と呼ばれます。

□ 新幹線は時速約300キロで走ります。

□ 新幹線は時速約300キロで走ります。たとえば、東京と福岡を約5時間で結びます。

□ 1964年に導入されて以来、全国の新幹線網は拡大しています。

□ 新幹線網は南は九州の鹿児島から、北は北海道まで延びています。

□ 日本を賢く楽しむには新幹線と在来線を利用することです。乗り換えも便利です。

□ 新幹線と在来線を利用すれば、ほとんど全国どこへでも行けます。

□ 新幹線には各駅に停車するものと、主要駅だけに停車するものがあります。

□ 東京から関西、九州方面へ行くには、のぞみという新幹線がもっとも速いです。［ひかりや各駅に停まるこだまもあります。］

□ 東京から東北、北海道方面へ行くには、はやぶさという新幹線が一番速いです。その他に多くの在来線も利用できます。

□ 東京から京都や大阪へ行きたいときは新幹線がおすすめです。

Shinkansen Bullet Trains and Railroads

Traveling in Japan by train is fun.

The Shinkansen is the name of the Japanese high-speed train.

Most major cities in Japan can be reached by high-speed trains called Shinkansen.

Shinkansen are often called bullet trains because of their shape.

The Shinkansen bullet train runs at a speed of about 300 kilometers per hour.

The Shinkansen bullet train runs at a speed of about 300 kilometers per hour. For example, it connects Tokyo and Fukuoka in about five hours.

Since its introduction in 1964, the Shinkansen bullet train network has expanded throughout Japan.

The Shinkansen bullet train network extends from Kagoshima in Kyushu in the south to Hokkaido in the north.

The best way to enjoy Japan wisely is to use both Shinkansen bullet trains and local lines. Transfers are also convenient.

You can go almost anywhere in Japan by using the Shinkansen bullet train and local lines.

Some Shinkansen bullet trains stop at every station, while others stop only at major stations.

The Nozomi Shinkansen bullet train is the fastest way to travel from Tokyo to Kansai and Kyushu. [There are also the Hikari and the Kodama, which stops at every station].

The Shinkansen bullet train called the Hayabusa is the fastest way to travel from Tokyo to Tohoku and Hokkaido. Many other local lines are also available.

If you want to go from Tokyo to Kyoto or Osaka, the Shinkansen bullet train is the way to go.

□ 東京、名古屋、京都、大阪間を移動するときは新幹線を利用するのが便利です。

□ 東京、名古屋、京都、大阪間を行き来するには、新幹線が便利です。各都市間を15分間隔で運行しています。

□ 混雑する時期を除けば、普通は駅に行って切符を買い、座席の予約なしでも新幹線に乗ることができます。

□ 日本人にとって新幹線は、旅するときの便利な移動手段であるだけでなく、海外への重要な輸出技術となっています。

□ 台湾は、海外で初めて日本の新幹線技術を導入して、高速列車システムを構築しました。

□ 日本の新幹線は、フランスのTGVやドイツのICEのようなものです。

The Shinkansen bullet train is a convenient way to travel between Tokyo, Nagoya, Kyoto, and Osaka.

The Shinkansen bullet train is a convenient way to travel between Tokyo, Nagoya, Kyoto, and Osaka. Trains run between each city every 15 minutes.

Except during busy periods, it is usually possible to go to the station, buy a ticket, and board the Shinkansen bullet train without a seat reservation.

For Japanese people, the Shinkansen bullet train is not only a convenient means of transportation when traveling, but also an important export technology.

Taiwan was the first overseas country to introduce Japanese Shinkansen technology to build a high-speed train system.

Japan's Shinkansen bullet train is like France's TGV or Germany's ICE.

日本食を楽しむ

Enjoying Japanese Cuisine

（☞ Sushi *p.73*）

Edomae, sushi
江戸前寿司

Popular sushi ingredients
人気が高い寿司ネタ

Uni, sea urchin ovaries, wrapped in *nori* seaweed in a style known as *gunkan maki*, or "battleship wrap"
ウニ（ウニの卵巣。海苔の巻きかたを「軍艦巻き」と言う）

Toro, a fatty cut of tuna
トロ（マグロの身の脂の多い部位）

Ebi, shrimp/prawns, either raw or boiled
エビ（生のエビと茹でたエビがある）

Anago, conger eel served simmered
アナゴ（うなぎの仲間で、煮て使う）

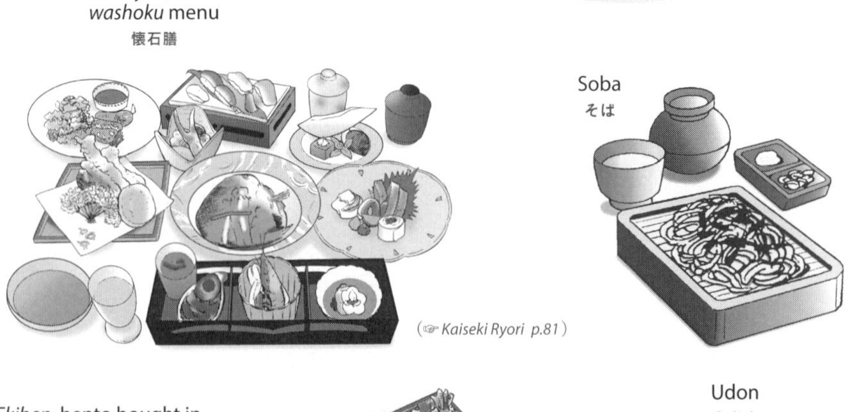

Kaisekiryori, refined *washoku* menu
懐石膳

（☞ *Kaiseki Ryori p.81*）

Soba
そば

Ekiben, bento bought in railway stations
駅弁

Makunouchi bento, traditional bento that was once eaten while watching *kabuki*
幕の内弁当

（☞ *Ekiben* / Bento *p.93*）

Udon
うどん

（☞ Soba and Udon, *p.85*）

Yosenabe, a kind of Japanese bouillabaisse
寄せ鍋

(☞ *Nabe p.79*)
(☞ Sukiyaki and *Shabu-Shabu p.77*)

Sukiyaki, a kind of Japanese fondue
すき焼き

Oden, a kind of Japanese stew
おでん

Shabushabu, a kind of Japanese fondue
しゃぶしゃぶ

Yakitori-ya
焼き鳥屋

(☞ *Yakitori p.81*)

Okonomiyaki-ya
お好み焼き屋

Kanto style, customers cook it themselves
関東風（客が自分で焼く）

Kansai style, prepared by chef
関西風（店員が焼いてくれる）

(☞ *Okonomiyaki p.91*)

日本食を楽しむ

旅の楽しみはなんといっても食事です。和食は、無形文化遺産にも登録され、世界の人にも人気です。寿司だけではない日本食を説明できるようになりましょう。

導入

□ 日本食は寿司だけではありません。

□ 日本食といってもいろいろな料理があります。

□ 寿司だけでも、多くの種類があります。

□ 海外の日本食レストランでは、幅広い日本食を出します。

□ 海外の日本食レストランでは、幅広い種類の日本食を出しますが、日本では違います。

□ 日本のレストランは、店によって専門料理が違います。

□ 日本食は日本語で和食といいます。

□ 日本の食べ物は和食といい、西洋の食べ物は洋食といいます。

刺身

□ 刺身はとても新鮮な生の魚です。

□ 刺身は世界で最も良く知られた日本の魚料理の一つです。

□ 刺身は生の魚を薄く切って、きれいに盛り付けたものです。

□ 刺身はいろいろな魚介でつくります。

Track 06

Introduction

Sushi is not the only type of Japanese food.

There are many different kinds of Japanese food.

Sushi alone comes in many varieties.

Japanese restaurants overseas serve a wide range of Japanese foods.

Japanese restaurants overseas serve a wide variety of Japanese foods, but this is not the case in Japan.

Japanese restaurants specialize in different cuisines depending on the restaurant.

Japanese cuisine is called *washoku* in Japanese.

Japanese food is called *washoku*, and Western food is called *yoshoku*.

Sashimi

Sashimi is very fresh raw seafood.

Sashimi is one of the best-known Japanese seafood dishes in the world.

Sashimi is thinly sliced raw seafood nicely displayed on the plate.

Sashimi can be made from a variety of seafood.

□ 刺身をつくるには、魚のさばき方や薄く切る技術が必要です。

□ 刺身はわさびと一緒に醤油につけて食べます。

□ 日本の寿司屋で、美味しくて新鮮な刺身を味わうことができます。

□ 刺身には日本語で「つま」という細く切った大根が添えられます。

□ 刺身には日本酒がよく合います。

寿司

□ 寿司は酢飯を使った日本食です。

□ 日本にはいろいろな寿司があり、地域ごとに伝統的な寿司があります。

□ 訪日した外国人がいう寿司は、一般的にはにぎり寿司のことで、寿司の中で最も人気があります。

□ 最も人気がありよく知られているのがにぎり寿司で、世界中の日本食レストランで出されています。

□ にぎり寿司は江戸前寿司ともいわれます。それは、封建時代に東京の旧名であった江戸で進化したからです。

□ にぎり寿司は楕円形ににぎった酢飯に刺身をのせたものです。

□ ちらし寿司は、酢飯の上に刺身や野菜、キノコ、玉子などの具をのせた寿司のことです。

□ いなり寿司も寿司の一種で、丸めた酢飯を油揚げで包んだものです。

□ 巻物とはのりで巻かれた寿司のことで、中身はマグロやキュウリなどです。

To make sashimi, one must have the skill to handle the fish and cut it into thin slices.

Sashimi is eaten dipped in soy sauce with *wasabi*.

You can taste delicious, fresh sashimi at Japanese sushi restaurants.

Sashimi is served with thinly sliced *daikon* radish called *tsuma* in Japanese.

Sake goes well with sashimi.

Sushi

Sushi is a Japanese dish made with vinegared rice.

There are various types of sushi in Japan, and each region has its own traditional sushi.

Generally, what foreign visitors call sushi is called *nigirizushi* in Japan. *Nigirizushi* is the most popular kind of sushi.

The most popular and well-known type of sushi is *nigirizushi*, which is served in Japanese restaurants around the world.

Nigirizushi is also known as *Edomaezushi*. This is because it evolved in Edo, the old name for Tokyo during the feudal era.

Nigirizushi is sushi with oval-shaped vinegared rice topped with sashimi.

Chirashizushi is sushi with sashimi, vegetables, mushrooms, eggs, and other ingredients on top of vinegared rice.

Inarizushi is another type of sushi, consisting of rolled sushi rice wrapped in fried tofu.

Makimono is a type of sushi wrapped in *nori* (seaweed) and filled with tuna, cucumber, etc.

□ 鉄火巻きは巻物の一種で、マグロを使って作ります。

□ かっぱ巻きは巻物の一種で、キュウリを使って作ります。

□ 太巻きとは、かんぴょう、椎茸、玉子焼きなどをのりで巻いてつくる寿司の一種です。

□ 5つ星の寿司屋はとても高いです。

□ 回転寿司は寿司屋のファストフードで気軽に寿司を味わえます。

□ 回転寿司では、いろいろな種類の寿司が小さな皿にのって、ベルトの上を廻っています。

□ 回転寿司では、会計の時に店員がテーブルの上の皿の数を数えます。皿の色によって値段が違います。

□ 寿司を食べる時は、あまり醤油をつけすぎないように注意しましょう。

□ 寿司を食べるには、箸を使うことも指でつまむこともできます。

□ アメリカには、カリフォルニアロールのような巻き寿司がいろいろあります。

Tekkomaki is a type of *makimono* made with tuna.

Kappamaki is a type of *makimono* made with cucumber.

Futomaki is a type of sushi made with *kanpyo* (dried gourd), *shiitake* mushrooms, and *tamagoyaki* (fried egg), wrapped in *nori*.

Five-star sushi restaurants are very expensive.

Kaitenzushi is a fast-food sushi restaurant that offers a casual sushi experience.

In *kaitenzushi*, various kinds of sushi are served on small plates and rotated on a belt.

At a *kaitenzushi* restaurant, the waiter counts the number of plates on the table when you pay. The price depends on the color of the plate.

When eating sushi, be careful not to put too much soy sauce on it.

To eat sushi, you can use chopsticks or pick it up with your fingers.

In the US, there are a variety of sushi rolls, such as the California roll.

回転寿司店の様子

天ぷら

□ 天ぷらとは、魚介や野菜を揚げたものです。

□ 天ぷらは、魚介や野菜を揚げたもので、衣は小麦粉と水でつくります。

□ たいていの魚介類は天ぷらにできます。とりわけ、海老の天ぷらはとても人気があります。

□ 美味しい天ぷらを食べるには、必ず新鮮な材料を使って揚げますが、揚げ過ぎてはいけません。

□ 天丼は、丼に入ったご飯の上に天ぷらをのせたものです。

□ 天ぷらは天つゆと一緒に出されます。

□ 天つゆは、魚だし、醤油、甘口の調理酒であるみりんでつくります。

すき焼き・しゃぶしゃぶ

□ すき焼きはテーブルの上で調理する鍋料理です。主な材料は薄く切った牛肉、豆腐、ネギ、キノコ、しらたきです。

□ すき焼きは鍋料理で、主な材料は薄く切った牛肉、豆腐、ネギです。浅い鉄鍋に、醤油、砂糖、みりん、酒を加えて調理します。

□ すき焼きは別皿に入った生卵につけて食べます。

□ しゃぶしゃぶは鍋料理で、主な材料は紙のように薄く切った牛肉です。

□ しゃぶしゃぶは鍋料理で、紙のように薄く切った牛肉を、豆腐や野菜などと一緒に食べます。

□ しゃぶしゃぶを楽しむには、薄く切った牛肉を熱い出汁に入れ、たれにつけて食べます。

□ レストランのランクに関わらず、しゃぶしゃぶは客が調理します。

Tempura

Tempura is deep-fried seafood and vegetables.

Tempura is deep-fried seafood or vegetables, and the batter is made of flour and water.

Most seafood can be made into tempura. Shrimp tempura, in particular, is very popular.

For good tempura, always use fresh ingredients and deep fry them, but do not fry them too long.

Tendon is a bowl of rice topped with tempura.

Tempura is served with tempura sauce called *tentsuyu*.

Tentsuyu is made with fish stock, soy sauce, and *mirin*, or sweet cooking sake.

Sukiyaki and *Shabu-Shabu*

Sukiyaki is a hot-pot dish cooked on the table. The main ingredients are thinly sliced beef, tofu, scallions, mushrooms, and *shirataki* noodles.

Sukiyaki is a one-pot dish, consisting mainly of thinly sliced beef, tofu, and green onions. It is prepared in a shallow iron pot with soy sauce, sugar, *mirin*, and sake.

Sukiyaki is served with a raw egg in a separate dish for dipping.

Shabu-shabu is a one-pot dish, the main ingredient being paper-thin slices of beef.

Shabu-shabu is a one-pot dish in which paper-thin slices of beef are served with tofu and vegetables.

To enjoy *shabu-shabu*, thinly sliced beef is placed in hot broth and dipped in sauce.

Regardless of the restaurant's rank, *shabu-shabu* is cooked by the customer.

□ 美味しいすき焼きやしゃぶしゃぶの高級店は、和牛を出します。

鍋物

□ おでんは冬に食べる人気の鍋料理です。ゆで卵、大根、さつま揚げ、こんにゃくといった材料を醤油の出汁で煮込んだものです。

□ ちゃんこ鍋は相撲部屋で出される鍋料理です。

□ ちゃんこ鍋は元々相撲取りによって作られた日本の鍋料理です。多くのお相撲さんが引退後にちゃんこ鍋屋を開きます。

□ 湯豆腐は、鍋に昆布を敷いて、そこに豆腐と水を入れて温めて食べる料理です。

□ 湯豆腐は豆腐を使う鍋料理で、冬の人気料理です。

□ 一般的な鍋料理では、具を食べた後に、残った出汁にご飯やうどんを入れて食べます。

和牛

□ 和牛は柔らかいことで有名です。

□ 和牛とは最高級の日本の牛肉で、柔らかいことで有名です。

□ 神戸と松阪は高品質の和牛で有名です。他にも多くの地域で独自の高級和牛を育てています。

Upscale restaurants serving good sukiyaki and *shabu-shabu* serve premium Japanese beef called *wagyu*.

Nabe (Hot-pot)

Oden is a popular hot-pot dish eaten in winter. Ingredients such as boiled egg, *daikon* radish, processed fish cakes, and *konnyaku*, or food made from the konjac plant, are boiled in soy-sauce-flavored broth.

Chankonabe is a hot-pot dish served in sumo stables.

Chankonabe is a Japanese hot-pot dish originally made by sumo wrestlers. Many sumo wrestlers open *chankonabe* restaurants after they retire.

Yudofu is a dish made by placing *kombu* (kelp) in a pot and heating tofu and water in it.

Yudofu is a popular winter hot-pot dish that uses tofu.

In a typical hot-pot dish, after the ingredients are eaten, rice or udon noodles are added to the remaining broth.

Wagyu (Premium Japanese Beef)

Wagyu, or premium Japanese beef, is famous for its tenderness.

Wagyu is the highest quality Japanese beef and is famous for its tenderness.

Kobe and Matsusaka are famous for the high quality of their premium Japanese beef. Many other regions raise their own high-quality premium Japanese beef.

焼き鳥

□焼き鳥とは鳥肉を串焼きしたものです。

□焼き鳥には多くの種類があります。鶏は皮や内臓を含め、ほとんどの部位が焼き鳥に使われます。

□鳥肉だけでなく野菜と組み合わせる食べ方もあります。

□つくねとは鶏の肉団子のことです。

□焼き鳥は屋台や居酒屋で出されるのがほとんどですが、中には品質にこだわった高級店もあります。

□焼き鳥は、ビールや日本酒とよく合います。

会席・懐石料理

□会席料理とは、高級な和食のフルコースです。

□会席料理の店では、いろいろな日本料理を最も洗練された形で楽しむことができます。

□会席料理は正式な食事で、宴席などで供されます。

□会席料理は決まったコースの中から選びます。単品の注文はできません。

□会席料理の店では、それぞれの料理が一品ずつ順番に出てきます。

□懐石は、お茶を美味しく味わうための食事で、本来は茶室で出されていました。

□もともと懐石は茶会前に出される料理で、「茶懐石」ともいわれます。

□日本料理は、調理法も種類もさまざまです。

□典型的な料理は、刺身、焼き魚、天ぷら、お吸いもの、野菜の煮物などです。

Yakitori (Grilled Chicken Skewers)

Yakitori is grilled chicken meat on a skewer.

There are many types of *yakitori*. Almost all parts of the chicken are used for *yakitori*, including the skin and internal organs.

It can be eaten not only with chicken meat, but also with vegetables.

Tsukune are chicken meatballs.

Most *yakitori* places are street vendors and casual bars, but there are some expensive *yakitori* restaurants specializing in high-quality chicken.

Yakitori goes well with beer or sake.

Kaiseki Ryori (Banquet Food) and *Kaiseki Ryori* (Tea Ceremony Food)

Kaiseki cuisine is a full course of high-class Japanese food.

At a *kaiseki* restaurant, you can enjoy a variety of Japanese cuisine in its most refined form.

Kaiseki ryori is a formal meal and is served at banquets.

Kaiseki cuisine is served in a set course. It is not possible to order individual dishes.

At a *kaiseki* restaurant, each dish is served in turn, one at a time.

Kaiseki is a meal for savoring green tea, originally served in a tea room.

Kaiseki was originally served before a tea ceremony and is also called *chakaiseki*.

Japanese cuisine varies in preparation and variety.

Typical dishes include sashimi, grilled fish, tempura, soup, and vegetable stew.

□日本料理は舌だけでなく目も楽しませてくれます。

□日本料理は見た目が重要で、すべての素材が美しく盛り付けられています。

□日本料理では季節ごとの素材が使われ、見た目の美しさだけでなく旬の味を楽しむことができます。

うなぎの蒲焼き・うな重

□うなぎは淡水魚で、濃厚なたれを付けて焼くこともあります。

□うなぎ料理は、うなぎの専門店で出されるのが一般的です。

□うなぎの蒲焼きは単に蒲焼きともいい、うなぎに特製のたれを付けて焼いたものです。

□日本人は夏にうなぎを食べます。うなぎは暑さに打ち勝つ精力をつけると信じられているからです。

□蒲焼きは魚を開いて骨を取り除いてから、串に刺し濃厚なたれを付けて焼きます。

□蒲焼きのたれは醤油、みりん、砂糖、酒などを混ぜたものです。

□うなぎの蒲焼きは江戸の郷土料理で、日本人の好物です。

□うなぎには豊富なタンパク質、脂肪、ビタミンA、Eが含まれています。

□うなぎの専門店では蒲焼きのほかにうな重が人気です。

□うな重とは、ご飯の上に蒲焼きをのせたものです。

□うなぎ料理には、肝吸いがよくついてきます。うなぎの内臓を入れた汁物です。

Japanese cuisine is a feast for the eyes as well as the palate.

Appearance is important in Japanese cuisine, and all ingredients are beautifully presented.

In Japanese cuisine, seasonal ingredients are used, allowing diners to enjoy not only the beauty of the appearance, but also the flavors of the season.

***Unagi no Kabayaki* (Broiled Eel) and *Unaju* (Grilled Eel on Rice)**

Eels are freshwater fish and are sometimes grilled with a rich sauce.

Eel dishes are usually served at restaurants specializing in eels.

Unagi no kabayaki, also known simply as *kabayaki*, is grilled eel with a special sauce.

Japanese people eat eels in summer. This is because eels are believed to give one energy to overcome the heat.

For *kabayaki*, the fish is opened, its bones are removed, and then it is skewered and broiled with a thick sauce.

The sauce is a mixture of soy sauce, *mirin*, sugar, and sake.

Kabayaki is a local delicacy of Edo (present-day Tokyo) and a favorite of the Japanese people.

Eel is rich in protein, fat, and vitamins A and E.

In addition to *kabayaki*, *unaju* (grilled eel on rice) is popular at eel specialty restaurants.

Unaju is a dish of broiled eel on a bed of rice.

Eel dishes are often accompanied by liver soup. This is a soup containing the internal organs of the eel.

そば・うどん

□ そばとは、そば粉でできた細い麺です。

□ 日本にはそば専門のそば屋という店があります。

□ もりそばとは、ざるに盛った冷たいそばです。

□ ざるそばとは、ざるに盛って海苔をかけた冷たいそばです。

□ 天ざるは天ぷらがついた冷たいそばです。

□ かけそばは熱いつゆをかけたそばです。

□ そばには熱い汁と一緒に出てくるものがあります。

□ うどんは小麦粉でつくる太めの麺で、食べ方はそばと似ています。

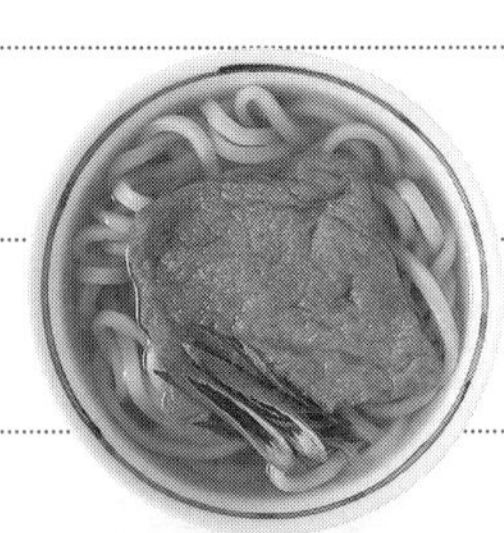

□ そばもうどんも、つけ汁に付けて食べる冷たいものと、だし汁がかかった温かいものがあります。

□ 西日本の人たちはそばよりもうどんをよく食べます。

□ 東日本の人たちはうどんよりもそばをよく食べます。

□ 日本人はよく麺をすすります。

□ 麺を食べるとき、日本では音をたてても構いません。

Track 07

Soba and Udon

Soba is thin noodles made from buckwheat flour.

In Japan, there are restaurants specializing in soba.

Morisoba is cold soba served in a draining basket.

Zarusoba is cold soba served in a draining basket and topped with seaweed.

Tenzaru is cold soba served with tempura.

Kakesoba is soba with hot sauce.

Some soba is served with hot soup.

Udon is thicker noodles made of wheat flour and eaten in a similar way to soba.

Both soba and udon can be served cold with dipping sauce or hot with broth.

People in western Japan eat udon more often than they eat soba.

People in eastern Japan eat soba more often than they eat udon.

Japanese people often slurp their noodles.

In Japan, it is acceptable to make noise when eating noodles.

ラーメン

□ ラーメンは日本で大人気のファストフードです。

□ ラーメンの起源は中国ですが、日本は独自の味に進化させました。

□ ラーメンは値段も手頃で、手軽な食べ物です。

□ ラーメンは日本で最も人気のある麺類の一つです。

□ 日本にはラーメン屋という専門店が無数にあります。

□ 大都市では、ラーメン屋はほとんど街角ごとにあります。

□ ラーメンのスープはさまざまな素材からつくります。

□ ラーメンのスープは、鶏、豚、魚、昆布、キノコ、野菜など、さまざまな素材からつくります。

□ ラーメンの麺は小麦粉でつくられます。

□ ラーメンは安価で手軽な食べ物ですが、有名店に定期的に通うような熱狂的なファンもいます。

□ 最も人気のあるラーメンの種類には、味噌、塩、醤油があります。

□ ラーメンには、味噌ラーメン、塩ラーメン、醤油ラーメンなどの種類があります。

□ 九州のラーメンは、豚骨でスープをつくる豚骨ラーメンです。

□ 札幌の味噌ラーメンは、バターをのせて食べることもあります。

□ ラーメンの典型的なトッピングは、チャーシュー、海苔、メンマ、ネギなどです。

Ramen

Ramen is a very popular fast food in Japan.

Ramen originated in China, but Japan has evolved its own unique flavor.

Ramen is affordable and easy to eat.

Ramen is one of the most popular types of noodle dishes in Japan.

There are countless ramen specialty shops in Japan.

In large cities, ramen shops can be found on almost every street corner.

Ramen broth is made from a variety of ingredients.

Ramen broth is made from a variety of ingredients, including chicken, pork, fish, kelp, mushrooms, and vegetables.

Ramen noodles are made of wheat flour.

Ramen is inexpensive and easy to prepare, but it also has a devoted following that regularly visit famous restaurants.

The most popular types of ramen include miso, salt, and soy sauce.

The different types of ramen include miso ramen, salty ramen, and soy sauce ramen.

In Kyushu, almost all ramen is served with a pork broth, and such ramen is called *tonkotsu* ramen.

Sapporo's miso ramen is sometimes topped with butter.

Typical ramen toppings include pork, seaweed, fermented bamboo shoots, and green onions.

カレーライス

□ カレーライスは人気の洋食です。

□ カレーはインドの料理ですが、日本人は19世紀終わりに独自のものを作りました。

□ 日本のカレーライスは、ご飯の上にカレーソースをかけたものです。

□ カレーライスは日本人に最も人気のある料理の一つです。

□ カレーライスとラーメンは、日本で最も人気のあるファストフードです。

□ 都会には多くのカレーライス専門店があります。

□ カレーライスは家庭でもよく作られます。

□ カレーライスには具材によって多くの種類があります。

□ ビーフカレーや、豚カツと組み合わせたカツカレーも日本人には人気があります。

豚カツ

□ 豚カツは豚肉に衣をつけて揚げたものです。

□ 豚カツ店ではヒレやロース肉を揚げたものを手頃な
値段で食べることができます。

Curry Rice

Curry and rice is a popular Western dish.

Curry is an Indian dish, but the Japanese created their own version at the end of the 19th century.

Japanese curry and rice is rice topped with curry sauce.

Curry and rice is one of the most popular dishes among Japanese people.

Curry and rice and ramen are the most popular fast foods in Japan.

There are many restaurants specializing in curry and rice in cities.

Curry and rice is often prepared at home.

There are many types of curry and rice, depending on the ingredients.

Beef curry and curry with pork cutlet are also popular among Japanese people.

Tonkatsu (Pork Cutlets)

Tonkatsu is deep-fried pork cutlets.

Tonkatsu restaurants offer deep-fried fillets and *rosu*, or pork-loin cutlet, for a reasonable price.

焼きそば・焼きうどん

□ 焼きそばは中華麺を油で炒める料理で、特製ソース、野菜、豚肉を加えることが多いです。

□ 焼うどんは焼きそばのようなものですが、使う麺はうどんです。

お好み焼き

□ お好み焼きは日本のピザのようなものです。

□ お好み焼きは関西で人気の料理です。

□ お好み焼き屋では、お好み焼きのほかに焼きそばも出します。

□ ピザと同じように、お好み焼きのトッピングも魚介から肉までさまざまです。

丼もの

□ 日本にはいろいろな丼ものがあります。

□ 丼ものは日本で人気のファストフードです。

□ 人気の丼料理は、親子丼、カツ丼、天丼、牛丼です。

□ 親子丼は鶏肉、玉ねぎを煮て、卵でとじ、ご飯にのせた料理です。

□ カツ丼は親子丼に似ていますが、鶏肉ではなく豚カツを使います。

□ 天丼はご飯の上に天ぷらをのせ、たれをかけたものです。

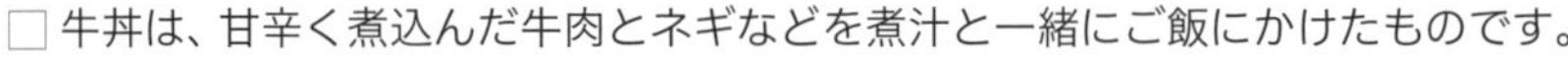

□ 牛丼は、甘辛く煮込んだ牛肉とネギなどを煮汁と一緒にご飯にかけたものです。

Yakisoba (Stir-Fried Soba Noodles) and *Yaki Udon* (Stir-Fried Udon Noodles)

Yakisoba is a food made of Chinese noodles stir-fried in oil, often with the addition of special sauce, vegetables, and pork.

Yaki udon is like *yakisoba*, but the noodles used are udon.

Okonomiyaki (Japanese pancakes)

Okonomiyaki is like Japanese pizza.

Okonomiyaki is a popular dish in the Kansai region.

In addition to *okonomiyaki*, *yakisoba* is also served at *okonomiyaki* restaurants.

Like pizza, toppings for *okonomiyaki* vary from seafood to meat.

Donburi (Rice-Bowl Dishes)

There are many rice-bowl dishes available in Japan.

Rice-bowl dishes are popular fast foods in Japan.

Popular rice-bowl dishes are *oyakodon*, *katsudon*, *tendon*, and *gyudon*.

Oyakodon is a dish made by simmering chicken and onions, wrapping it in egg, and serving it over rice.

Katsudon is similar to *oyakodon*, but it uses pork cutlet instead of chicken.

Tendon is a bowl of rice topped with tempura and sauce.

Gyudon is sweet and spicy beef stewed with green onions and other ingredients served over rice.

弁当

□ 弁当はご飯やおかずを箱に詰めて持ち運べるようにしたものです。

□ 弁当は丁寧にお弁当といわれることもあります。

□ 弁当は学校や仕事先での昼ご飯、ピクニック、旅行や法事の席などでも食べます。

□ 弁当スタイルの料理を出すレストランもあります。

□ 高級な和食レストランでは、漆塗りの美しい箱に食材を詰めたミニ懐石を出すところもあります。

□ 弁当は盛り付けが美しいことで広く知られています。

駅弁

□ 駅弁とは列車の駅で売られている弁当のことです。

□ 列車に長く乗るのであれば、駅弁という特別な弁当を試すいいチャンスです。駅弁は主要駅で販売されています。

□ 駅弁には地元の特産物が入っていることが多いです。

おにぎり

□ おにぎりは、ご飯を三角や丸形にしたものです。

□ おにぎりを作るときは、塩を少し掌に振ってから握ります。

□ 多くの場合、おにぎりはご飯の中に具を入れて握ったものを海苔で包みます。

□ おにぎりは持ち歩くのに適しているので、どこでも食べることができます。

Bento

A bento is rice and side dishes packed in a box for carrying.

Bento is sometimes politely referred to as *obento.*

Bento are eaten for lunch at school or work, on picnics, on trips, or at memorial services.

Some restaurants serve bento-style food.

Some upscale Japanese restaurants serve miniature *kaiseki* meals with ingredients packed in beautifully lacquered boxes.

Bento are widely known for their beautiful presentation.

Ekiben (Station Bento)

Ekiben are bento sold at train stations.

If you take a long ride on a train, you will have the opportunity to try a special type of bento called *ekiben*, which is sold in main stations.

Ekiben often contain local specialties.

Onigiri (Rice Balls)

Onigiri are rice balls made in a triangular or round shape.

When making an *onigiri*, a little salt is sprinkled on the palm of the hand before it is made.

In most cases, *onigiri* are made by placing the ingredients in the rice and wrapping the rice ball in seaweed.

Onigiri are suitable for carrying around and can be eaten anywhere.

調味料・日本食の用語

□ 味噌とは大豆を発酵させたペースト状のものです。

□ 納豆は大豆を発酵させたもので、よくご飯にのせて食べます。

□ みりんとは甘い調理酒です。

□ 海苔は海藻の一種を干したもので、とくに朝食時にご飯と一緒に食べます。

□ 大根おろしとは大根をすり下ろしたものです。

□ 胡麻だれとは胡麻味のソースでしゃぶしゃぶや冷たいうどんなどを食べるときに使います。

□ ポン酢とは柑橘果汁を入れた醤油で、刺身やしゃぶしゃぶなどに使います。

□ 梅干しは梅の実を塩漬けして干した食品で、酸っぱいですが健康にいいです。

□ わさびは、日本の辛味（調味料）でペースト状のものもあります。

□ 鰹節とはカツオを煮て燻してから乾燥させた保存食品です。
削って出汁や料理の味付けに使います。

わさび

日本茶

□ 日本茶は日本語でお茶といいます。

□ 日本茶は緑茶として知られています。

□ 日本人は緑茶のことをお茶と呼び、レストランでは水と同じで無料です。

□ お茶はふつうは温かいものです。

□ ペットボトルに入った冷たいお茶は自動販売機で買えます。

Seasonings and Japanese Food Terms

Miso is fermented soybeans.

Natto is fermented soybeans and is often eaten over rice.

Mirin is sweet cooking sake.

Nori is dried laver, and it is eaten with rice, particularly at breakfast.

Daikon oroshi is grated *daikon* radish. *Daikon* is Japanese radish.

Goma-dare is a sesame-flavored sauce used for *shabu-shabu*, cold udon, and so on.

Ponzu is soy sauce with citrus juice and is used for sashimi, *shabu-shabu*, etc.

Umeboshi is a food made by pickling and drying pickled plums in salt. It is sour but healthy.

Wasabi is a Japanese spice (seasoning) that is also available in paste form.

Katsuobushi are a preserved food made by boiling and smoking bonito before drying. It is shaved and used to flavor soup stock and dishes.

Japanese Tea

Japanese tea is called *ocha* in Japanese.

Japanese tea is known as green tea.

Japanese people call green tea "*ocha*," and it is free of charge in restaurants, just like water.

Ocha is typically served hot.

Cold tea in plastic bottles can be purchased from vending machines.

□ 日本には様々な種類のお茶があります。

□ 茶会で点てられるお茶は抹茶という粉末状のもので、日常で出されるお茶とは違います。

□ 日本茶といえば一般的には緑茶の一種である煎茶のことで、抹茶とは違います。

□ 煎茶は、茶葉を急須に入れてお湯を注いでから飲みます。

□ 玉露とは苦みが少なく、甘くてコクのある高級なお茶です。

□ 番茶とは夏が過ぎてから摘まれた茶葉で淹れるお茶のことです。

□ ほうじ茶とは焙煎した茶葉で淹れるお茶です。香ばしくてさっぱりしています。

□ 玄米茶とは茶葉に炒った玄米を混ぜたお茶です。

和菓子

□ 日本の伝統的な菓子を和菓子といいます。

□ 和菓子はお茶と一緒に出されることが多いです。

□ 和菓子はお茶と一緒に出されることが多いです。和菓子を先に食べてからお茶を飲むのは、苦味を和らげお茶の味を引き立ててくれるからです。

□ 和菓子は茶会でも供されます。

□ 見た目も美しい和菓子は、茶会の席には欠かせないものです。

□ あんことは、小豆を煮て砂糖を加えて練ったものです。

□ あんこを生地で包んだ和菓子が数多くあります。

There are many types of tea in Japan.

The tea served at tea ceremonies is made from powdered *matcha*, which is different from the tea served in everyday life.

Japanese tea is generally *sencha*, which is one type of green tea and different from *matcha*.

Sencha is drunk after the tea leaves are placed in a teapot and hot water is poured over them.

Gyokuro is a high-grade tea that is sweet and full-bodied with little bitterness.

Bancha is tea brewed with tea leaves picked after summer.

Hojicha is tea brewed from roasted tea leaves. It is fragrant and refreshing.

Genmaicha is tea made by mixing roasted brown rice with tea leaves.

***Wagashi* (Traditional Japanese Sweets)**

Traditional Japanese confections are called *wagashi*.

Wagashi is often served with tea.

Wagashi is often served with tea. The reason for eating *wagashi* first and then drinking tea is that it lessens the bitterness and enhances the flavor of the tea.

Wagashi is served at tea ceremonies too.

Wagashi, with their beautiful appearance, are an indispensable part of the tea ceremony.

Anko is made by boiling *azuki* beans and kneading them with sugar.

There are many *wagashi* made by wrapping *anko* in dough.

□ 和菓子のつくり方や飾りには、季節感があふれています。

□ 生菓子とは、主にあんこを使った水分の多い柔らかい和菓子です。

□ 饅頭は生菓子の代表例です。

□ 饅頭は、生地であんこを包んで蒸したものです。

□ 落雁は、水分の少ない乾燥した菓子である干菓子の一種で、型にはめて作ります。

□ 干菓子の中でも人気なのが煎餅です。

□ 煎餅は練った米粉を焼いて、しょう油や塩で味付けしたものです。

□ 日本にはいろいろな干菓子がありますが、甘いものばかりではなく、塩からいものから辛いもの、香ばしいものもあります。

Wagashi are made and decorated to give a strong sense of the season.

Namagashi is a soft, moist *wagashi* made mainly with red bean paste.

Manju is a typical example of *namagashi.*

Manju is made by wrapping sweet bean paste in dough and steaming it.

Rakugan is a type of *higashi* (a type of dry confectionary) that is made by molding it into shapes, and is characterized by its low water content and dry texture.

Senbei rice crackers are one of the most popular dried confections.

Senbei are made of kneaded rice flour, baked, and seasoned with soy sauce and salt.

There are many kinds of dried confections in Japan, not only sweet ones, but also salty, spicy, and savory ones.

酒

- □酒は米から造る日本の伝統的なアルコール飲料です。

- □酒を造るには、米、水、麹を使った複雑な工程があります。

- □酒のことを英語で「ライスワイン」と言うこともありますが、アルコール度数もワインと同じくらいです。

- □酒は、冷やにも、常温にも、ぬる燗にも、熱燗にもできます。

- □酒は、冷やにも、常温にも、ぬる燗にも、熱燗にもできます。その温度によって酒の味わいも変わってきます。

- □酒の美味しい飲み方は銘柄や季節によって変わります。

- □暑くて湿気の多い夏場は、冷やが爽快ですし、寒い冬の夜には熱燗こそがおすすめです。

- □酒は種類によって味が異なります。自分の好みで、甘口から辛口まで選ぶことができます。

- □ワインと同じように、酒も大手メーカーだけでなく、地方特有の小規模な醸造所もたくさんあります。

- □地方にある醸造所の酒は地酒といわれ、とても人気があります。

- □醸造所ごとに異なる手法で酒を造ります。そのため、辛口から甘口までさまざまな酒が味わえます。

- □大きな百貨店や酒屋には、日本中の醸造所で造られたいろいろな銘柄があります。

Track 08

Sake

Sake is a traditional Japanese alcoholic beverage made from rice.

Making sake is a complex process that involves rice, water, and mash.

Sake is sometimes called "rice wine" in English and has the same alcohol content as wine.

Sake can be served cold, at room temperature, lukewarm, or hot.

Sake can be served cold, at room temperature, lukewarm, or hot. The flavor of sake changes depending on the temperature.

The best way to drink it depends on the brand and the season.

In the hot and humid summer months, cold sake is refreshing, and on cold winter nights, hot sake is the way to go.

Sake tastes different depending on the type. You can choose anything from sweet to dry varieties based on your preference.

Like wine, sake is not only made by major manufacturers, but there are also many small breweries that are unique to local regions.

Sake from local breweries is known as *jizake* and is very popular.

Each brewery uses a different method to make their sake. As a result, you can taste a wide variety of sake, from dry to sweet.

Large department stores and liquor stores carry a wide variety of brands made at breweries throughout Japan.

□ 純米酒とはアルコールを使わず、米と米麹だけで造る酒のことです。

□ 本醸造酒とは、70％以下に精米した白米を使った酒のことです。

□ 吟醸酒は、よりすっきりとした味わいの酒を造るために、60％以下に精米した白米を使います。

□ 大吟醸酒は、50％以下に精米した白米を使った上質な酒です。

□ 生酒とは、いっさい加熱処理をしていない酒のことです。

□ ワインテイスティングのように、利き酒という酒の味見も面白い経験となるでしょう。

□ ぬる燗や熱燗で酒を飲むときは、陶製の徳利と猪口という器を使います。

□ 冷酒は普通、ガラスのコップで飲みます。

□ 常温の酒を飲むときは、木製の升という器を使います。

□ 杉でできた升のいい匂いで、酒の味が引き立ちます。

□ 酒は料理の際にも、味を深めるために使われます。

□ 酒は神道にとっても重要な意味を持つ飲み物です。

□ 酒は神に供えられるので、神道の儀式では聖水と見なされています。

□ 神に供える酒をお神酒（みき）といいます。

□ 日本人の友人と一緒であれば、酒やビールを相手のコップに注いであげるのは普通のことです。

Junmai sake is sake made without alcohol, using only rice and rice malt.

Honjozo sake is a type of sake made with refined white rice that has been polished to 70% or less of its original size.

Ginjo sake is made from white rice polished away to 60 percent or less of its original size in order to produce a drink with a more refreshing taste.

Daiginjo sake is a high quality sake made from white rice polished to 50% or less of its original size.

Namazake is sake that has not been heat-treated at all.

Like wine tasting, sake tasting is an interesting experience.

When drinking lukewarm or hot sake, ceramic cups called *tokkuri* and *choko* are used.

Chilled sake is usually served in a glass.

When sake is drunk at room temperature, it is served in wooden cups called *masu*.

The good smell of the wooden cups made of cedar enhances the taste of sake.

Sake is also used to enhance the flavor of food.

Sake is also an important drink in Shinto.

Sake is considered a sacred beverage in Shinto rituals because it is offered to the spirits.

The sake offered to the gods is called *omiki*.

If you are with your Japanese friends, it is common practice to pour sake or beer into their glasses.

□ 一緒に飲んでいる相手に酒を注ぐ習慣をお酌といいます。

□ 最初の一杯を飲み始めるときは「乾杯！」といいます。

□「乾杯」とは、杯の酒を飲み干すという意味です。

□ 日本では乾杯したときに、中国のように酒を飲み干す必要はありません。

焼酎

□ 焼酎は日本の蒸留酒で、米、麦、芋、黒糖などから造られます。

□ 酒と同様、日本中に焼酎の蒸留所が多数あります。

□ 鹿児島県はサツマイモで造る焼酎で有名です。

□ 泡盛は沖縄の有名な焼酎で、地元の米で造ります。

□ 黒糖で造る焼酎は、日本の南の島々で人気があります。

□ 焼酎をベースにした焼酎カクテルも人気で、いろいろな種類が楽しめます。

□ 伝統的に焼酎はお湯割りで飲まれていました。

□ 昨今、焼酎をロックで飲むのが流行っています。

The custom of pouring sake into the cup of the person you are drinking with is called *oshaku*.

When one starts drinking the first glass, one says, "*Kanpai*!" (Cheers!)

Kanpai means to drink up the sake in the cup.

In Japan, it is not necessary to finish all the sake when toasting, unlike in China.

Shochu (Japanese Distilled Spirits)

Shochu is a Japanese distilled spirit made from rice, barley, sweet potatoes, brown sugar, and other ingredients.

As with sake, there are many local *shochu* distilleries all over Japan.

Kagoshima Prefecture is famous for *shochu* made from sweet potatoes.

Awamori, Okinawa's famous *shochu*, is made from local rice.

Shochu made from brown sugar is popular in the southern islands of Japan.

Shochu cocktails based on *shochu* are also popular, and many different types are available.

Traditionally, *shochu* was drunk with hot water.

Nowadays, it is popular to drink *shochu* on the rocks.

＼ちょこっと／

知っておきたい日本紹介のコツ❷

● 固有名詞の発音

外国の人に地名や、固有名詞を説明するときは、できるだけゆっくり、そしてはっきりと発音しましょう。ほとんどの固有名詞は日本語です。日本語は一見発音が簡単だと思いがちですが、中には「りょう ryo」や「つ tsu」など、外国人が苦手な音の組み合わせもあるのです。例えば、お隣の韓国の人たちの場合、「ざ行」や「つ」の発音はなかなか思うようにいきません。こうしたことを理解して、海外からの人に接するのも小さな気配りといえるでしょう。

● まずは自分の知識から

日本人以外の人に、日本のことを説明するときは、まず説明したいことについて、自分自身の知識をしっかりとまとめておくことも大切です。普段何気なく使っている言葉も、それを説明するとなると、結構知らないことも多いものです。特に「日本人気質」といった抽象的な概念は、日本語で説明するのも至難の業です。本書で英文フレーズを読みながら、自分の言葉でどう説明できるのかを考え、時にはまず日本語の文章にしてみることも大切です。日本語で説明できないことを、英語で説明することはできません。

● 日本についての知識

例えば、一般のアメリカの人たちが日本のことを知る機会がどれだけあるかといえば、それは極めて限られています。アメリカの教科書で日本が本格的に取り上げられるのは、ペリーの来航、第二次世界大戦、戦後の同盟関係といったところでしょうか。そのため、日本の名所旧跡で、ただそのいわれや概略を話しても、相手からみれば何のことやらということも多々あるでしょう。

例えば、大阪城を説明するとき、豊臣秀吉について語ることは必須ですね。しかし、おそらく多くの外国人は豊臣秀吉のことを知りません。この場合、「日本にも内乱の続いた時期がありました。それは16世紀のことです（We had also a civil war period in Japan. It was 16th century.)」のように、世界に共通する「civil war」という話題からはじめ、「豊臣秀吉は当時の英雄で日本を統一した人です（He was known as the man who united Japan at that time.)」などとつなげると良いでしょう。

第 ③ 章

日本の四季と生活

季節と生活

習慣とマナー

日本の四季

Four Seasons

Kagami mochi, decorations of rice cakes for New Year
鏡餅

Kadomatsu, traditional decorations of New Year
門松 *p.113*

Karuta, a traditional card game
カルタ *p.115*

Hinaningyo, traditional dolls for the festival for girls
ひな人形 *p.119*

Hanami, cherry blossom viewing
花見 *p.121*

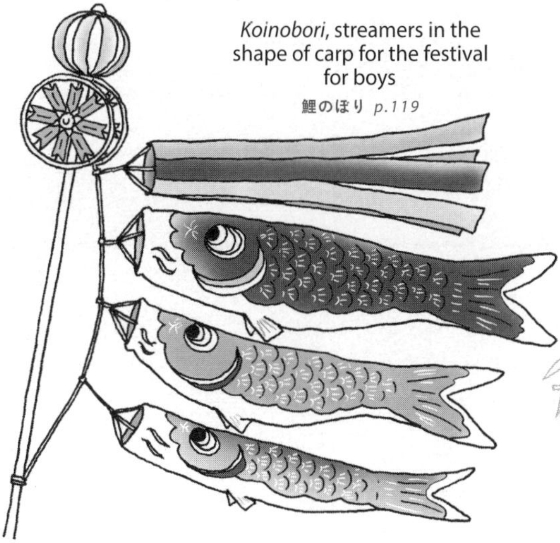

Koinobori, streamers in the shape of carp for the festival for boys
鯉のぼり *p.119*

Tanabata, the festival of constellation legend
七夕 *p.123*

Otsukimi, the full moon viewing
お月見 *p.127*

Ochugen, mid-summer gifts
Oseibo, year-end gifts
お中元・お歳暮 *p.127*

Shichi-Go-San, the festival for children aged 3, 5 and 7
七五三 *p.127*

季節と生活

お正月の過ごし方から、花見、節句、お彼岸、お月見、そしてクリスマスから大晦日と、日本の１年を四季をおって紹介します。

四季

□ 日本の生活や習慣は、季節の移り変わりと深くかかわっています。

□ 日本は農業国だったので、人々の生活は季節の移り変わりに強く影響されました。

□ 日本は温帯にあるので、四季の変化が明瞭です。そのことが人々の生活や習慣にも深くかかわっています。

□ 世界の多くの場所がそうであるように、日本でも季節の移り変わりに応じて、さまざまな行事や祭りが行われます。

□ 日本の行事や祭りには、地域に古くから伝わる言い伝えや風習の影響が色濃く残っています。

正月

□ お正月とは、新年のことです。

□ 新年を迎えて初めて人と会ったときは、「明けましておめでとうございます」と言います。

□ お正月とは新年を意味し、日本人にとっては最も重要な祝日です。

□ 日本人は、12月末から1月初旬の間に休暇を取ります。

□ 日本人は、12月末から1月初旬の間に休暇を取り、お正月を家族と過ごします。

Track 09

Seasons

Japanese life and customs are deeply intertwined with the changing seasons.

Since Japan was an agricultural country, people's lives are strongly influenced by the changing seasons.

Since Japan is in the temperate zone, there are four distinct seasons. This has deeply influenced people's lifestyles and customs.

As in many other places in the world, various events and festivals are held in Japan based on the changing of the seasons.

Japanese events and festivals are strongly influenced by local traditions and customs that have been handed down from generation to generation.

New Year's

Oshogatsu is New Year's.

When we meet people for the first time after the New Year, we say, "*Akemashite omedeto gozaimasu.*"

Oshogatsu means "New Year's" and it is the most important holiday season for Japanese people.

Japanese people take a vacation between the end of December and the beginning of January.

Japanese people take a vacation between the end of December and the beginning of January to spend New Year's with their families.

正月の習慣

□ お正月には、日本人は伝統的な習慣に従います。

□ 初詣とは、新年になって初めて社寺に参拝することです。

□ 年賀状とは新年を祝って交換されるはがきのことです。

□ 年賀状は新年を祝って書き送るはがきのことですが、最近ではメールやSNSで年賀状の代わりにする人が多くなっています。

□ 新年に初めて仕事をすることを仕事始めといいます。1月4日から働き始めるところが多いです。

□ 初荷とは、年が明けて初めて出荷される荷物のことです。昔はトラックに幟を立てるなどして荷物を運びました。

□ 門松とは、お正月を迎えるために家の前に置かれる竹と松で作られた伝統的な飾りのことです。

□ 注連縄飾りとは、藁と紙でできた特別な正月飾りのことで、邪気を払うために玄関に飾ります。

New Year's Customs

During New Year's, Japanese people follow traditional customs.

Hatsumode is the custom of visiting Shinto shrines at the beginning of the year.

Nengajo are postcards exchanged to celebrate New Year's.

Nengajo are postcards written to celebrate the New Year, but nowadays many people are using e-mail and social networking services in place of them.

The first day of work in the New Year is called *shigotohajime* (beginning of work), and many places begin work on January 4.

Hatsuni means "first freight," and in old times these loads were delivered in trucks on which special flags were raised to celebrate the New Year.

Kadomatsu are traditional decorations made of bamboo and pine branches used to welcome the New Year.

Shimenawa decorations are special New Year's decorations made of straw and paper that are placed at a home's entrance to ward off evil spirits.

初詣（湯島天神・東京都）

正月の料理

□ おせち料理とは、お正月用に特別に調理され重箱に詰められた食べ物です。

□ 伝統的に日本人はお正月には家族とおせち料理を食べます。おせち料理とは、お正月用に特別に調理され重箱に詰められた食べ物です。

□ 日本人はお正月には、重箱に詰められたおせち料理と餅を食べます。

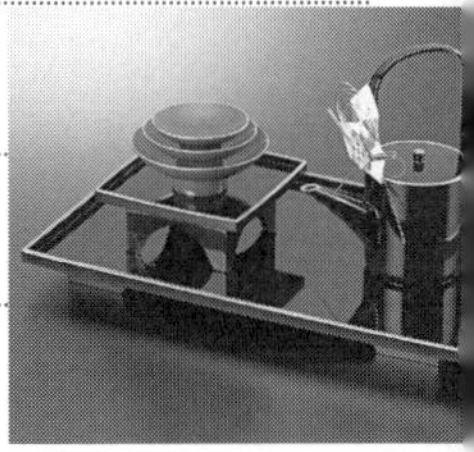

□ 日本人はお正月に、お屠蘇（とそ）という薬酒を飲みます。

□ 一般的に、お正月は1月7日までです。

□ 一般的に、お正月は1月7日までです。その日は、春の七草を刻んで入れたお粥を食べます。その粥は、七草がゆと呼ばれます。

正月の遊び

□ お正月には伝統的に、男の子は凧揚げを楽しみます。

□ 百人一首とは、お正月に行われるカードゲームです。中世の有名な歌人100人によって詠まれた和歌の上の句と下の句を合わせる遊びです。

□ お正月に、子どもたちはカルタという伝統的なカードゲームを楽しみます。女の子は羽根つきをします。

□ 羽根つきはバドミントンのようなもので、お正月の女の子たちの遊びです。

□ 羽根つきに使われるラケットは羽子板といい、美しく装飾されたものもあります。

New Year's Dishes

Osechi ryori is food specially prepared and packed in stacked boxes for the New Year.

Traditionally, Japanese people eat *osechi ryori* with their families on New Year's Day. *Osechi ryori* is food specially prepared and packed in stacked boxes for the New Year.

Japanese people eat *osechi ryori* in stacked boxes and rice cakes during the New Year.

Japanese people drink a kind of medicinal sake called *otoso* during the New Year.

Traditionally, the New Year's period ends on January 7.

Traditionally, the New Year's period ends on January 7, when people eat rice soup made using seven types of spring greens. This rice porridge is called *nanakusa-gayu*.

New Year's Games

Traditionally, boys enjoy flying kites during New Year's.

Hyakunin isshu is a New Year's card game in which the players have to match upper and lower parts of a *waka* poem created by 100 celebrities of the medieval period.

During New Year's, children enjoy a traditional card game called *karuta*. Girls play *hanetsuki*, a Japanese game of shuttlecock.

Hanetsuki is like badminton and is a New Year's game for girls.

The racket used for *hanetsuki* is called a *hagoita*, and some are beautifully decorated.

節分

□節分とは、春の始まりとされる立春の前日のことです。

□１年を健やかに過ごせるようにと、節分の日には豆まきをする習慣があります。

□節分の日には、厄除けや福を呼び込むという意味で豆まきをする習慣があります。

バレンタインデー

□日本では2月14日のバレンタインデーにチョコレートを贈るのが一般的です。

□日本のバレンタインデーの特徴は、女性から男性にチョコレートを贈ることが多いです。

□バレンタインデーにチョコレートを贈る習慣は、日本の製菓会社が始めたとされています。

□チョコレートは好きな人にだけでなく、職場の上司や同僚、学校の友人にも贈ります。

□職場の上司や同僚に贈るチョコレートは、「義理チョコ」と呼ばれます。義理で贈るチョコレートという意味です。

□3月14日のホワイトデーは、男性が女性にお菓子を贈るとされています。この習慣も製菓会社の販売戦略で始まったものです。

お彼岸

□春分の日と秋分の日の前後7日間を、日本では「お彼岸」と呼びます。

□お彼岸の間、人々は先祖のお墓参りをして、感謝の気持ちを伝えます。

□春分の日と秋分の日は国民の祝日です。日本人は故郷に帰って、家族と一緒にお墓参りをします。

Setsubun (Bean Throwing Festival)

Setsubun is the day before *risshun*, the beginning of spring.

On *Setsubun*, there is a custom of throwing beans to pray for a healthy year.

On *Setsubun*, it is customary to throw beans to ward off bad luck and bring in good fortune.

Valentine's Day

In Japan, it is common to give chocolates on Valentine's Day, February 14.

Valentine's Day in Japan is unique because women usually give chocolates to men.

The custom of giving chocolates on Valentine's Day was started by Japanese confectionery companies.

Chocolates are given not only to the person you love, but also to your bosses at work, colleagues, and school friends.

Chocolates given to bosses and colleagues at work are called *giri-choko*. It literally means obligation chocolate.

On White Day, March 14, men are supposed to give sweets to women. This custom also started as a sales strategy by confectionery companies.

Ohigan (The Equinoxes)

The seven days around the vernal equinox and the autumnal equinox are called *Ohigan* in Japan.

During *Ohigan*, people visit the graves of their ancestors to express their gratitude.

Vernal Equinox Day and Autumnal Equinox Day are national holidays. Japanese people return to their hometowns and visit graves with their families.

桃の節句・端午の節句

□ 節句は、古代中国からきた習慣であり、3月と5月の節句では、子どもたちの健康と将来を祝います。

□ 3月3日は女の子、5月5日は男の子の節句です。

□ 3月3日は、桃の節句と呼ばれています。太陰暦で桃の花が咲く季節だからです。

□ 3月3日の節句は女の子のためのもので、親は階段状の台に雛人形を飾ります。

□ 雛人形は平安時代の宮中の儀式を模した人形です。この習慣により、3月3日の節句を「雛祭り」とも呼びます。

□ 5月5日は端午の節句と呼ばれ、男の子のためのものです。

□ 端午の節句の頃、男の子がいる家では、鯉を模したのぼりを戸外に立てて、男の子が元気に強く育つことを願います。

□ 鯉のぼりとは鯉を模した管状の吹き流しで、5月5日の男の子の節句を祝うものです。

□ 端午の節句に男の子の成長を祝って、伝統的な侍の人形やミニチュアの兜を飾ります。

***Momo-no Sekku* and *Tango-no Sekku* (Peach Festival and Dragon Boat Festival)**

Sekku are a custom that originated in ancient China. The March and May festivals celebrate the health and future of children.

The *Sekku* festival on March 3 is for girls, and the one on May 5 is for boys.

March 3 is called *Momo-no Sekku* (Peach Festival). This is because it is the season when peach blossoms bloom, according to the lunar calendar.

The March 3rd *Sekku* is for girls, and parents display *hina* dolls on a staircase-like stand.

Hina ningyo are dolls modeled after ceremonies at the court of the Heian period. Due to this custom, the March 3rd *Sekku* is also called *Hinamatsuri.*

May 5 is called *Tango-no Sekku* and it is for boys.

During *Tango-no Sekku*, households with boys erect streamers in the shape of carp outside their homes in the hope that the boys will grow up strong and healthy.

A *koinobori* is a tubular streamer in the shape of a carp, and is used to celebrate the Boys' Festival on May 5.

During the Dragon Boat Festival, we celebrate the growth of boys by decorating traditional samurai dolls and miniature helmets.

桜と花見

□ 桜の花は、日本では春のシンボルです。

□ 桜の花はわずか1週間くらいしかもちません。

□ 日本人は桜の開花を春到来のしるしにしています。

□ 桜の開花日をカウントダウンするために、日本人は天気予報で「桜前線」という言葉を使います。

□ 桜前線とは、開花日が等しい地点を結んだ線のことで、南から北へと日本列島を移動します。

□ 桜前線とは、桜が開花する前線のことです。それは南から北上してくる春の到来を象徴するものです。

□ 春は南から北上してくるので、日本人は桜の開花を春の到来であると見なします。

□ 一般的に、桜前線は3月の終わりに九州に到達します。そして、日ごとに日本列島を北上していきます。

□ 日本人は桜の花の下でピクニックを楽しむことが好きです。

□ 日本人は桜の花を見ながら宴会を楽しみます。この習慣を日本語で「花見」といいます。

Cherry Blossoms and Blossom Viewing

Cherry blossoms are a symbol of spring in Japan.

Cherry blossoms last only about a week.

Japanese people see the opening of cherry blossoms as an indication that spring has arrived.

To count down the days until the blooming of cherry blossoms, the Japanese use the word *sakura-zensen*, or cherry blossom front, in weather forecasts.

The cherry blossom front refers to the line that connects points with the same blooming date, moving from south to north across the Japanese archipelago.

The cherry blossom front is the front line along which the cherry blossoms bloom. It symbolizes the arrival of spring moving northward from the south.

Since spring moves northward from the south, Japanese people regard the blooming of cherry blossoms as the arrival of spring.

Typically, the cherry blossom front reaches Kyushu at the end of March. It then moves northward through the Japanese archipelago day by day.

Japanese people love to enjoy picnics under the cherry blossoms.

Japanese people enjoy feasts while viewing cherry blossoms. This custom is called *hanami* in Japanese.

ゴールデンウィーク

□ ゴールデンウィークとは4月末から5月初旬にかけての期間のことで、何日かの休日が続きます。

□ ゴールデンウィークには、日本人は仕事を休んで休暇を楽しみます。

□ ゴールデンウィークは晩春の時期であり、天気がとてもよく、多くの人が家族や友だちと外で時間を過ごします。

□ ゴールデンウィーク中は、電車、飛行機、高速道路など、とても混雑します。

衣替え

□ 衣替えとは、6月1日と10月1日にそれぞれ夏服と冬服に取り替える日本人の習慣のことです。

□ 多くの場合、衣替えは制服を着用しているところで行われます。

□ 衣替えは、ほとんどの学校、工場や百貨店などの制服を着用する職場で、年に2度行われます。

□ 家庭では季節に応じて服の収納場所を整理したり、時期が過ぎて片づける前に服の手入れをしたりします。

夏の風物詩

□ 夏になると日本人は、「ビアガーデン」と呼ばれる屋外や建物の屋上に設置された店でビールを楽しみます。

□ 夏には、仏教の儀式に基づいた伝統的な祭りが日本全国で開かれます。

□ 七夕は7月7日に行われる祭りで、星の伝説に基づいています。

Track 10

Golden Week

Golden Week is a period between the end of April and the beginning of May when there are several holidays in a row.

During Golden Week, Japanese people take time off from work to enjoy a vacation.

Since Golden Week is a period in late spring when the weather is quite good, many people spend time outside with their families and friends.

Trains, airplanes, and highways are very crowded during Golden Week.

Seasonal Clothing Replacements

Koromogae is the Japanese custom of replacing summer and winter clothing on June 1 and October 1, respectively.

In many cases, seasonal clothing replacements are done where uniforms are required.

Seasonal clothing replacements take place twice a year in most schools and in workplaces where uniforms are worn, such as factories and department stores.

At home, people organize their clothing storage areas according to the season and take care of their clothes before putting them away after the season has passed.

Summer

In summer, Japanese people enjoy beer in restaurants called beer gardens, which are set up outdoors or on the roofs of buildings.

Traditional festivals based on Buddhist rituals are held throughout Japan in the summer.

Tanabata is a festival held on July 7 and is based on a Zodiac legend.

□星座の伝説によると、愛する2人が天の川によって引き裂かれ、1年に1度、7月7日の七夕の間だけ会うことができるのです。

□七夕には竹を立てて、願い事を書いた細長い紙をその枝に結びつけます。

□全国高校野球大会は日本人に最も人気のある夏のイベントの1つです。

□毎夏、全国高校野球大会が甲子園球場で開催されます。

お盆

□お盆は夏に行われる伝統的な行事で、人々は家族と一緒にお墓参りに行きます。

□お盆は仏教の習慣に基づく重要な休日であり、日本人は先祖に敬意を表します。

□多くの人たちはお盆の間に1週間の休みを取り、家族と過ごします。

□お盆の時期になると、帰省する人が多いので、空港や駅などはとても混雑します。

□日本各地で、お盆に灯籠(とうろう)流しが行われます。

□灯籠流しとは、灯籠を川に流す行事のことです。その灯籠は、この1年以内に亡くなった人たちの魂を象徴したものです。

□8月15日は、第二次世界大戦の終戦記念日です。

□8月15日はお盆と第二次世界大戦の終戦記念日が重なります。

□8月15日は、第二次世界大戦の終戦記念日です。そして、この戦争中に300万人以上の兵士と民間人が亡くなったので、日本人にとっては非常に重要な日です。

A Zodiac legend says two lovers separated by the Milky Way can meet only once a year during *Tanabata* on July 7.

On *Tanabata*, a bamboo plant is used, and long, thin strips of paper with wishes written on them are tied to its branches.

The National High School Baseball Tournament is one of the most popular summer events among Japanese people.

Every summer, the national high school baseball tournament is held at the Koshien Stadium.

Obon

Obon is a traditional summer event during which people visit graves with their families.

Obon is an important holiday based on Buddhist custom, in which Japanese people pay their respects to their ancestors.

Many people take a week off during *Obon* to spend time with their families.

During the *Obon* season, airports and train stations become very crowded as many people return home.

Lantern floating ceremonies are held in many parts of Japan during the *Obon* season.

Lantern floating is an event in which lanterns are floated down a river. The lanterns symbolize the souls of those who have died within the past year.

August 15 is the anniversary of the end of World War II.

August 15 coincides with *Obon* and the anniversary of the end of World War II.

August 15 is the anniversary of the end of World War II. It is a very important day for Japanese people because more than three million soldiers and civilians died during the war.

秋の風物詩

□日本では、秋は読書やスポーツを楽しむ季節であるといわれています。

□昔から日本人は、9月中旬の満月を見ることをとても好みました。この習慣は日本語で「月見」といいます。

□太陰暦では、菊を楽しむ季節は9月でしたが、西洋暦では10月になります。

□秋になって葉が色を変え始めると、日本人は山へ行ったり、京都などの伝統的な町を訪れます。

□秋になると、全国各地で収穫祭が行われます。

七五三

□七五三とは、11月15日に行われる7歳、5歳、3歳児を祝う年中行事で、男の子は5歳になったとき、女の子は3歳と7歳になったときに祝います。

□5歳になった男の子や3歳か7歳になった女の子が可愛らしい着物を着て家族と神社をお参りし、健康と将来の成功を祈ります。

お中元とお歳暮

□真夏と年末には、感謝の意を込めて贈りものを交わします。

□お中元とは、お世話になった人、仕事で付き合いのある人などに贈り物をすることです。

□お中元は、7月中旬から8月中旬までの間に贈られるのが一般的です。飲み物や果物、食品などが好まれます。

□お歳暮とは、助けてくれたり、気にかけてくれたりしてお世話になった人に、年末に贈り物をすることです。

□真夏や年末は、お中元やお歳暮があるため、日本のデパートにとって稼ぎ時です。

Autumn in Japan

In Japan, autumn is said to be the season for reading and enjoying sports.

Since ancient times, Japanese people have been very fond of viewing the full moon in mid-September. This custom is called *tsukimi* in Japanese.

According to the lunar calendar, the season for enjoying chrysanthemums was September, but according to the Western calendar, it is October.

In autumn, when the leaves begin to change color, Japanese people go to the mountains or visit traditional cities, such as Kyoto.

In autumn, harvest festivals are held all over Japan.

Shichi-Go-San

Shichi-go-san is the Seven, Five, and Three Festival held on November 15 for boys who have turned five years old and girls who have turned three or seven years old.

Boys who turned five years old or girls who turned three or seven years old visit Shinto shrines wearing cute kimonos and pray for their health and futures.

Ochugen and *Oseibo* (Mid-Summer and Year-End Gifts)

In midsummer and at the end of the year, gifts are exchanged as an expression of gratitude.

Ochugen is the giving of gifts to those who have taken care of us or those with whom we have business relationships.

Ochugen gifts are generally given between mid-July and mid-August. Beverages, fruits, and foods are preferred.

Oseibo is a gift given at the end of the year to those who have helped and cared for you.

Midsummer and year end are peak sales seasons for Japanese department stores because of *ochugen* and *oseibo.*

クリスマスと忘年会

□ クリスマスの時期になると、人々は買い物、食事、恋愛を楽しみます。

□ ほとんどの日本人にとって、クリスマスは宗教的なイベントではありません。

□ 12月になると多くの日本人は、忘年会という宴会を開きます。そこで飲んだり食べたりしてこの一年の締めくくりをします。

□ 忘年会とは日本人が年末に開く宴会のことで、お互いに感謝し合い、お酒や食事を楽しみます。

□ 仕事をしている人たちは、会社主催、部署主催、そして取引先との忘年会に参加するために忙しく、予定を合わせなければなりません。

大晦日

□ 12月31日は大晦日と呼ばれます。

□ 大晦日やその前日、日本人は大掛かりな家の掃除をします。これを「大掃除」といいます。

□ 新年を祝って書き送るはがきのことを年賀状といいます。年内に投函し、元日に届くことが大切です。

□ 大晦日の夜、多くの人は新年を迎える習慣としてそばを食べます。

□ 大晦日の真夜中ごろから、僧侶はお寺の鐘を108回つきます。

□ お寺の鐘を108回つく習慣は「除夜の鐘」と呼ばれ、108の煩悩を取り除き新年を迎えるという意味が込められています。

Christmas and *Bonenkai* (Year-End Parties)

At Christmas time, people enjoy shopping, eating, and romance.

For most Japanese people, Christmas is not a religious event.

In December, many Japanese people hold a party called a *bonenkai*. There, they drink, eat, and celebrate the end of the year.

Bonenkai are parties held by Japanese people at he end of the year to say thank you to one another and enjoy drinking and eating.

Workers are busy and have to adjust their schedules to attend year-end parties hosted by the company, by their departments, and with their business partners.

New Year's Eve

December 31 is known as New Year's Eve.

On New Year's Eve and the day before, Japanese people do extensive house cleaning. This is called *osoji*.

Postcards written to celebrate the New Year are called *nengajo*. It is important to post them within the year so that they will be received on New Year's Day.

On New Year's Eve, many people eat soba as a custom to welcome the New Year.

Around midnight on New Year's Eve, monks strike the temple bell 108 times.

The custom of striking the temple bell 108 times is called *joya no kane*, which means to remove 108 worldly desires that trouble humans and welcome the New Year.

習慣とマナー

日本の習慣やマナーを英語で説明できるようになりましょう。日本にしばらく滞在する人、ビジネスで駐在する人には有用な情報です。

家に招かれる

□ 日本人は家に入るとき靴を脱ぎます。

□ 日本人の家に入るときは靴を脱がなければなりません。

□ 家が伝統的であろうと現代的であろうと、日本人は家に入るとき靴を脱ぎます。

□ 伝統的な和室では、じかに床に座ります。

□ 伝統的な和室には椅子がなく、じかに床に座ります。

□ 座布団とは、座るための日本のクッションです。

□ 椅子に座る代わりに、日本人は座布団という平らなクッションのようなものに座ります。

□ 外国の人にとって、日本式に正座するのは辛いことでしょう。

□ あぐらとは、男性が足を組んで楽に座るやり方です。

□ 女性はあぐらではなく、正座の足を横に出して座ります。そうすれば足を休めることができます。

□ 日本人は居間でテレビを見るとき、ソファに座らないで床に座ることがあります。その方が楽だからです。

Track 11

Invitation to a House

Japanese people take off their shoes when they enter houses.

Shoes must be removed when entering a Japanese home.

Whether the house is traditional or modern, Japanese people take off their shoes upon entering.

In traditional Japanese rooms, people sit directly on the floor.

There are no chairs in a traditional Japanese room.

A *zabuton* is a Japanese cushion for sitting on.

Instead of sitting down in a chair, Japanese people seat themselves on a type of flat cushion called a *zabuton*.

For foreigners, it can be difficult to sit on the floor Japanese-style.

Agura is a way for men to sit comfortably with their legs crossed.

Rather than sitting crosslegged, women sit Japanese-style with their legs to the same side. This lets them rest their legs.

When watching TV in the living room, Japanese people often sit on the floor instead of on the sofa. This is because it is more comfortable.

座る位置

□ 日本人の家に招かれると、床の間を背にした席を勧められます。

□ 敬意を表すために、日本人は客に床の間を背にした上席に座るよう促します。

□ 会社を訪問すると、ドアとは反対側の奥の席を勧められます。

ビジネスマナー

□ 日本では、自己紹介の意味を込めて、最初に会ったときに名刺交換をします。

□ 肩書きや職場が変わってなければ、同じ人と次に会ったときに再び名刺交換する必要はありません。

□ 名刺を受け取るとき、両手で受け取るのが礼儀です。

□ 日本人相手に名刺を差し出すときは、最もタイトルの高い人に最初に手渡します。

□ 名刺を交換するとき、日本人は普通、丁寧にお辞儀します。

□ 相手が海外から来たことがわかっているときは、日本人もときには軽くお辞儀しながら握手することがあります。

□ 名刺はその人の顔であると考えられているので、相手の前で名刺をポケットに入れるのは、いいことではありません。

□ 受け取った名刺は、着席したデスクの上に丁寧に置きましょう。名刺の上下が逆さにならないよう気をつけます。

□ 日本人と話すときはファーストネームは使わない方がいいでしょう。

□ 日本人相手に話すときは、名字に「さん」をつけるのが一般的です。

□ 相手の会社を訪問したときは、促されるか相手が席に着くまで座らないことです。

Sitting Positions

When you are invited to a Japanese home, you will be asked to sit with your back to the *tokonoma*, or alcove.

As a sign of respect, the Japanese encourage their guests to sit on the seat of honor with their backs to the *tokonoma*, or alcove.

When visiting a company, a seat in the back opposite the door is recommended.

Business Manners

In Japan, business cards are exchanged at the first meeting as a way of introducing oneself.

Unless your title or workplace has changed, there is no need to exchange business cards again the next time you meet the same person.

When accepting a business card, it is polite to accept it with both hands.

When you give your name card to your Japanese counterparts, hand the first one to the person with the highest position.

When exchanging business cards, Japanese people usually bow politely.

When it is known that the person is from overseas, Japanese sometimes shake hands with a slight bow.

Since business cards are considered to be like people's faces, it is not a good idea to stuff them into one's pocket in front of others.

Place the business card you receive carefully on the desk where you are seated. Be careful not to turn the business card upside down.

When speaking to Japanese people, it is best not to use first names.

When speaking to a Japanese person, it is common to add san to the last name.

When you visit the office of your counterparts, do not sit down before you are asked to do so or until the host has taken a seat.

□ 仕事の打ち合わせで座るときには、足を組むことはおすすめできません。

□ 公式な会合の場では、両手を膝の上に乗せ、背筋をまっすぐにするのが普通です。

□ 仕事の打ち合わせのとき、日本人はよくコーヒーかお茶を出しますが、ホスト側が最初に口を付けてから飲むのが普通です。

お土産

□ 日本人は旅行したときに、お土産を買って渡す習慣があります。

□ お土産は、同僚や家族、親しい友人にも渡します。

□ お土産は空港や主要駅で購入することができます。典型的なお土産はチョコやクッキー、地方の珍味などです。

結婚式

□ 結婚式は神道かキリスト教の習慣に沿って行われるのが一般的ですが、ごくまれに仏式で行われることもあります。

□ ほとんどの場合、結婚式がカップルの信仰に基づいて行われることはありません。

□ 披露宴とは結婚パーティーのことで、ホテルや式場の宴会場で開かれます。

□ 披露宴で花嫁は、和装から洋装などにお色直しをします（その反対もあります）。

□ 披露宴に招かれたら、受付で署名し、贈り物としてお祝い金を渡します。

□ お祝いのお金は、祝儀袋という特別な贈答用の封筒に入れ、封筒に自分の名前を書きます。

When sitting down for a business meeting, crossing your legs is not recommended.

In formal meetings, it is normal to place your hands on your knees and keep your back straight.

During business meetings, Japanese people often serve coffee or tea, but it is normal for the host to sip it first before drinking it.

Souvenirs

Japanese people have the custom of buying and giving gifts called *omiyage* when they travel.

Souvenirs are given to colleagues, family members, and close friends.

Souvenirs can be purchased at airports and major train stations. Typical souvenirs include chocolate, cookies, and local delicacies.

Weddings

Weddings are usually held in accordance with Shinto or Christian customs, but very rarely as a Buddhist ceremony.

In most cases, weddings are not based on the couple's religious beliefs.

A *hiroen* is a wedding party and is held in a banquet hall at a hotel or wedding hall.

At the wedding reception, the bride changes from traditional Japanese clothing to Western-style clothing (or sometimes vice versa).

If you are invited to a *hiroen*, you need to sign your name at the reception area and give congratulation money as a gift.

The congratulatory money is placed in a special gift envelope called a *shugi-bukuro*, and your name is written on the envelope.

□ 結納式では、女性を花嫁として迎えるため、花婿の両親が花嫁の家を訪れ、両親に結納金をはじめとする祝いの品を贈ります。

葬式

□ 葬式は故人の家の信仰に基づいて行われます。

□ お通夜は葬式の前夜に行われます。

□ お通夜は葬式に似ていますが、式のあと故人の思い出を語り合うための食事があります。

□ 故人の家族と親しくなければ、食事の誘いを受ける必要はありません。

□ お通夜の翌日に、主たる葬儀（告別式）が執り行われます。

□ 告別式に出るときには、受付で署名し、香典という現金を収めます。

□ 仏式の葬儀の場合、棺が置かれた祭壇の前に行き、焼香して合掌します。

□ 焼香とは仏式の葬儀で行われる儀式のことで、香炉に細かくした香を入れてから合掌します。

冠婚葬祭

□ 冠婚葬祭は日本人の暮らしの中で最も重要な行事です。

□ 冠婚葬祭とは日本人にとって重要な4つの儀式のことです。その4つの儀式には成人式、結婚式、葬式、法事があります。

□ 成人式とは大人になったことを祝う儀式です。

At a *yuino* ceremony, the parents of the groom visit the parents of the bride-to-be and present gifts including money because they are receiving the new wife into their family.

Funeral

Funerals are held according to the beliefs of the deceased's family.

The *otsuya*, or wake, is held the night before the funeral.

A wake is similar to a funeral, but after the ceremony, there is a meal to share memories of the deceased.

If you are not close to the family of the deceased, you do not need to accept the invitation to eat.

Following the day of the wake, the main funeral ceremony takes place.

When you visit places where funeral ceremonies are held, you have to write your name at the reception area and give a gift of cash called a *koden*.

In a Buddhist-style funeral, one approaches the altar where the coffin is placed, offers incense, and joins one's palms together in prayer.

Shoko refers to a ritual performed during a Buddhist funeral, where one places finely ground incense into an incense burner and then joins one's palms together in prayer.

Kankonsosai (Weddings, Funerals, and Ceremonial occasions)

Weddings, funerals, and ceremonial occasions are the most important events in the lives of Japanese people.

Kankonsosai consists of four important ceremonies for Japanese people. They are the Coming of Age Ceremony, the wedding, the funeral, and the death-memorial ceremony.

Seijinshiki is a ceremony to celebrate becoming an adult.

□ 日本では、長い間20歳になると成人したと見なされていましたが、2022年に18歳に引き下げられました。

□ 1月の第２月曜日には、地域の役所が成人式を行います。

□ 成人の日は1月の第2月曜日で、成人した人たちを祝います。

□ 結婚の儀式のことを、日本語では結婚式といいます。

□ 多くの場合、結婚式は神式かキリスト教式で行われます。

□ 冠婚葬祭の「葬」とは、故人を弔うための葬儀のことです。

□ 葬儀の習慣、儀式は神式か仏式かで変わってきます。

□ 冠婚葬祭の「祭」とは、故人の命日に開かれる特別な集まりのことです。

□ 法事とは、仏式の特別な行事のことで、命日から一定の間隔で故人を弔うためにお祈りします。

□ 主な法事は、初七日（命日から数えて７日目）、四十九日（命日から数えて49日目）、一周忌（命日から１年後）、三回忌（亡くなってから２年経過した３年目）、七回忌（亡くなってから６年経過した７年目）が行われるのが一般的です。

□ 法事には僧侶が呼ばれ、故人への供養のためにお経をあげます。

In Japan, for a long time, reaching the age of 20 was considered adulthood, but this was lowered to 18 in 2022.

On the second Monday in January, local government offices hold a coming-of-age ceremony.

Coming of Age Day is the second Monday in January and celebrates those who have reached adulthood.

The marriage ceremony itself is called a *kekkon-shiki* in Japanese.

In most cases, weddings are performed in the Shinto or Christian style.

The *so* in *kankonsosai* is a memorial service for a person who has passed away.

The customs and rituals of the memorial service vary depending on whether it is a Shinto or Buddhist ceremony.

The *sai* in is a special memorial gathering on the anniversary of a person who has passed away.

A *hoji* is a special Buddhist ceremony in which prayers are offered to mourn the deceased at regular intervals from the anniversary of death.

Major Buddhist memorial services are usually held on the 7th day after a death, the 49th day after the death, on the 1st anniversary of the death, on the 3rd anniversary of the death, and on the 7th anniversary of the death.

In a Buddhist memorial service, a priest is called to perform a ritual offering to the deceased, reciting sutras to provide solace and sustenance for the deceased's spirit.

ちょこっと
知っておきたい日本紹介のコツ③

● Why に注意！

海外の人は、ごく軽い気持ちで Why で始まる質問をします。特に日本の事情を語るとき、わからないことがあれば、まず飛んでくるのが Why です。こうした場合、すぐに返答できる場合は Because などで応対します。もし、ちょっと考えなければ答えられないときは Well, などと言って対応しましょう。

● 海外の常識を利用しよう

例えば、「As you had the revolution in 1776, we had a similar situation around 1868.（ちょうどあなた方が 1776 年に革命を経験したように、我々も 1868 年に似たようなことがありました）」といえば、明治維新のことをアメリカ人たちにわかりやすく説明することができます。相手の国の歴史や常識を理解し、それを参考に日本を説明することも一つのテクニックです。

● 起承転結に注意！

日本人は英語でものごとを説明するときも、普段から慣れている起承転結法に従って話してしまいがちです。しかし、この論理構成は日本や韓国などでしか通用しません。欧米の人にものごとを説明するときは、必ず最も大切なポイントや結論を先に述べて、その理由などを後から解説するように努めましょう。

第4章

日本の伝統と文化

伝統芸能と芸術

現代文化・風潮

スポーツ

日本の伝統芸能 The Traditional Arts of Japan

Kabuki

歌舞伎
（☞ *Kabuki p.147*）

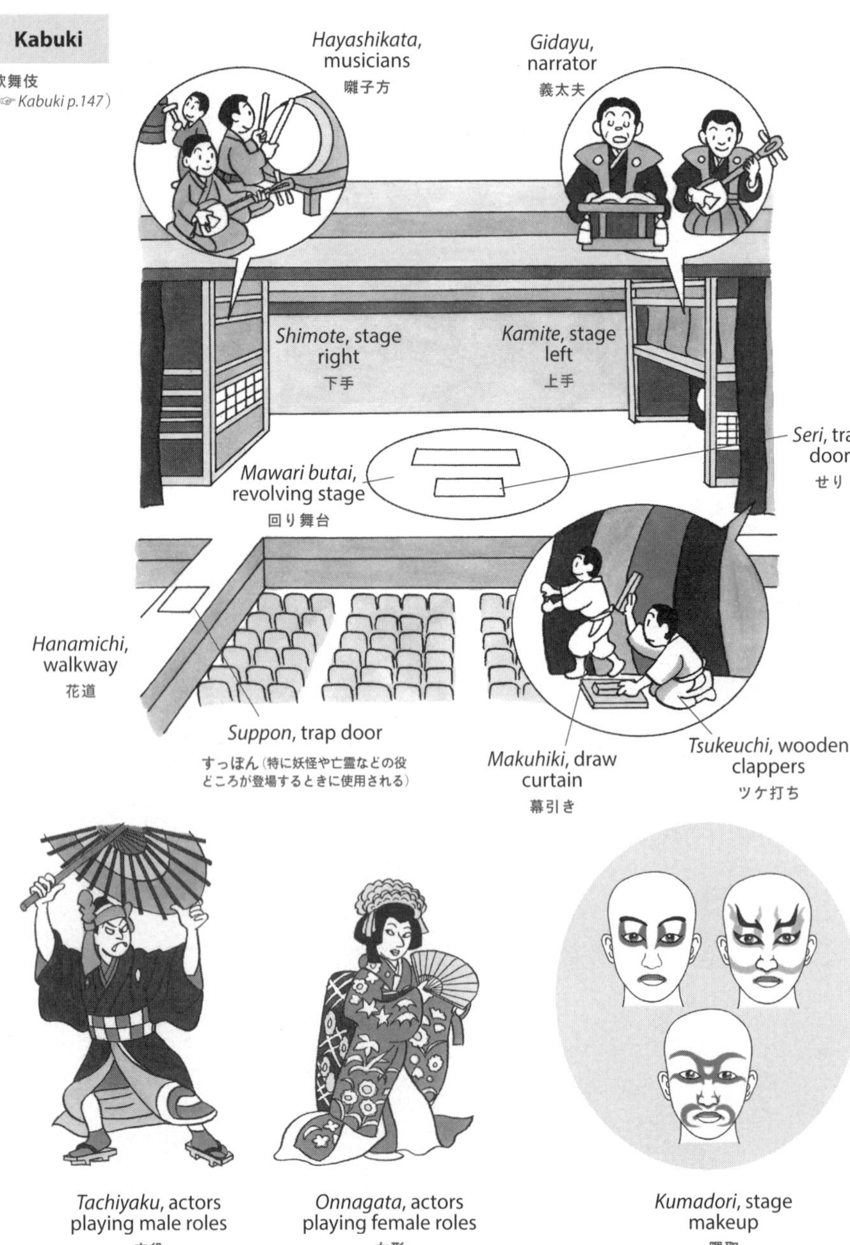

Tachiyaku, actors playing male roles
立役

Onnagata, actors playing female roles
女形

Kumadori, stage makeup
隈取

Noh Play

(☞Noh *p.153*)

能

Noh masks

面の一例

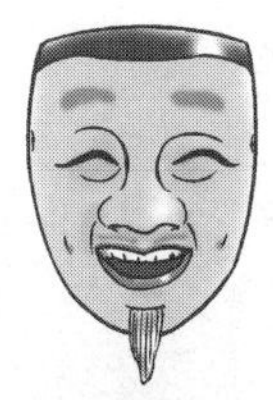

Enmeikaja, a mask denoting a god

延命冠者(神を表す面)

Koushijo, a dignified old man

小牛尉(品のある老人を表す面)

Hannya, a female vengeful spirit

般若(女性の怨霊を表す面)

Koomote, a young woman

小面(若い女性を表す面)

Noh Stage

能舞台

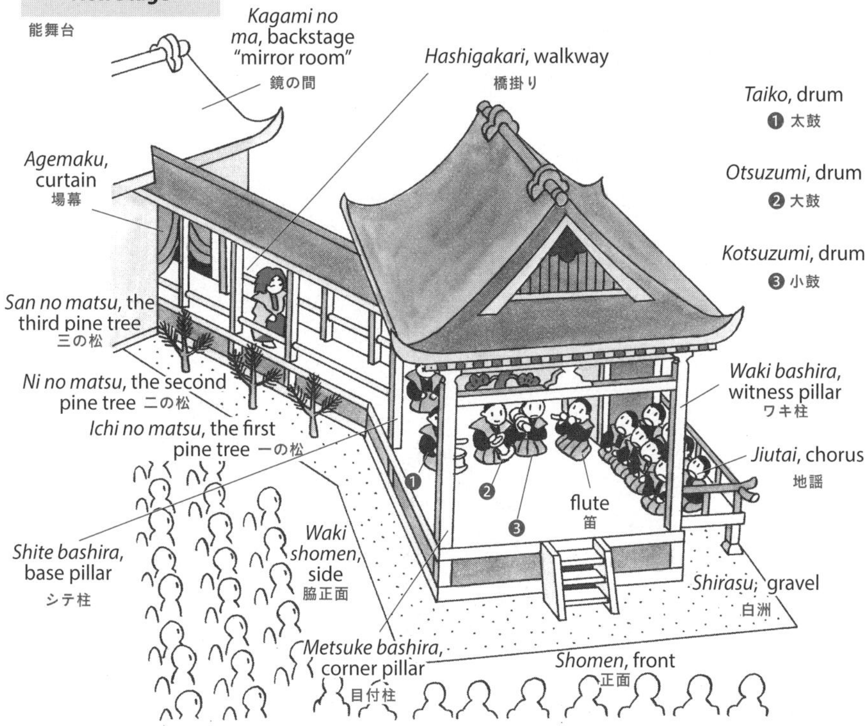

Kagami no ma, backstage "mirror room"
鏡の間

Hashigakari, walkway
橋掛り

Taiko, drum
❶ 太鼓

Otsuzumi, drum
❷ 大鼓

Kotsuzumi, drum
❸ 小鼓

Agemaku, curtain
揚幕

San no matsu, the third pine tree
三の松

Ni no matsu, the second pine tree 二の松

Ichi no matsu, the first pine tree 一の松

Waki bashira, witness pillar
ワキ柱

Jiutai, chorus
地謡

flute
笛

Shite bashira, base pillar
シテ柱

Waki shomen, side
脇正面

Shirasu, gravel
白洲

Metsuke bashira, corner pillar
目付柱

Shomen, front
正面

Bunraku

文楽

(☞ *Bunraku* p.151)

Omozukai, chief puppeteer, who controls the head and right arm

主遣い

(左手で人形の表情を、右手で人形の右手を操る。舞台下駄という大きな下駄を履いている)

Hidarizukai, left puppeteer, who controls the left arm

左遣い

(人形の左手を操る。黒衣を纏っている)

Ashizukai, leg puppeteer, who controls the feet

足遣い

(人形の下にうずくまり、両手で人形の両足を操る。黒衣を纏っている)

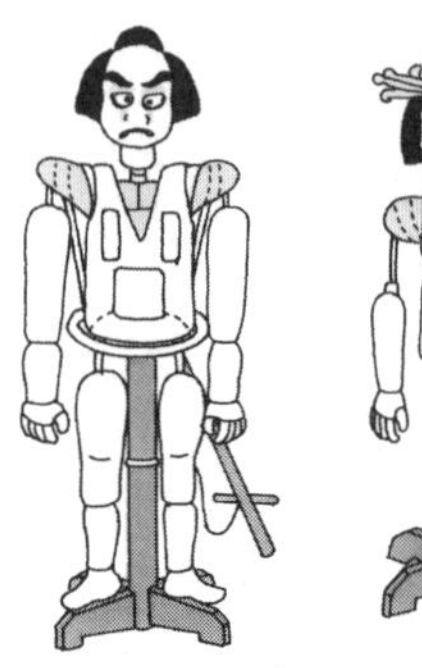

Bunraku puppets

文楽の人形

Wagakki, Japanese Instruments

和楽器

Koto, Japanese harp

琴

Shakuhachi, bamboo flute

尺八

Tsuzumi, small drum

鼓

Shamisen, Japanese three-string lute

三味線

相撲を知る

（☞Sumo Wrestling *p.173*）

Get to Know Sumo

Kuro-busa, black tassel, marks the northwest and symbolizes winter
黒房（北西に掛けられる。冬を表す）

Aka-busa, red tassel, marks the southeast and symbolizes summer
赤房（南東に掛けられる。夏を表す）

Shiro-busa, white tassel, marks the southwest and symbolizes autumn
白房（南西に掛けられる。秋を表す）

Higashi no hanamichi, eastern wrestlers' entrance
東花道

Ao-busa, green tassel, marks the northeast and symbolizes spring
青房（北東に掛けられる。春を表す）

Shio, salt
塩

Nishi no hanamichi, western wrestlers' entrance
西花道

Yobidashi, usher
呼出し
（力士を呼び出す人）

Chikaramizu, purifying and fortifying water
力水

Gyojidamari, referees' waiting place
行司だまり

Dohyo, ring
土俵

Shinpancho, chief judge
審判長

Shikiri-sen, start line
仕切り線

Gyoji, referee
行司

Yokozuna, the highest rank of sumo wrestler
横綱（力士の最高位）

Sekitori, sumo wrestlers in *makuuchi* or *juryo* classes
関取（十両以上の力士）

Makushita, sumo wrestlers ranked below *Juryo*
幕下（番付の２段目に書かれる力士。十両の一階級下）

Gyoji, referee
行司

伝統芸能と芸術

日本に来たら歌舞伎を見たい、という方もいらっしゃると思います。歌舞伎、文楽、能、狂言、そして日本古来の着物から茶道・華道の説明まで身につけることができます。

歌舞伎

□ 歌舞伎は日本特有の演劇です。

□ 歌舞伎は江戸時代に発展した日本特有の演劇です。

□ 歌舞伎は、能楽、人形浄瑠璃（文楽）と並んで、日本の三大国劇といわれています。

□ 歌舞伎は日本の伝統芸能の一つで、役者と演奏家が演じます。

□ 歌舞伎はバックで演奏される音楽に合わせて演じられます。

□ 歌舞伎はバックで演奏される音楽に合わせて演じられ、メインの楽器は三味線です。

□ 歌舞伎では、三味線、笛、太鼓の演奏をする人たちが座り、ときには長唄が歌われることもあります。

□ 今日の歌舞伎は日本の伝統的な舞台芸術で、演劇、踊り、音楽を一体化したものです。

□ 日本では、有名な歌舞伎役者は著名人で、しばしばテレビドラマなどにも出演します。

□ 異国情緒あふれる歌舞伎は、外国人にも人気があります。

□ 多くの外国人観光客は、歌舞伎役者の特徴のある化粧とパフォーマンスを楽しんでいます。

Track 12

新装の歌舞伎座

Kabuki

Kabuki is a Japanese performing art.

Kabuki is a Japanese performing art developed during the Edo period.

Kabuki is considered one of Japan's three major classical theater forms, along with noh and *ningyo joruri* (also known as *bunraku*).

Kabuki is one of Japan's traditional performing arts, and performed by actors and musicians.

Kabuki is performed with music played in the background.

Kabuki is performed to music played in the background, and the main instrument is the *shamisen*.

In *kabuki*, seated musicians play *shamisen*, flutes, and drums. Sometimes musicians sing songs called *nagauta*.

Today, *kabuki* is a traditional Japanese performing art form that integrates drama, dance, and music.

In Japan, famous *kabuki* actors are celebrities and often appear in TV dramas too.

Kabuki, with its exotic atmosphere, is also popular among foreigners.

Many foreign tourists enjoy the *kabuki* actors' distinctive makeup and performances.

□ 異国情緒あふれる踊り、音楽、衣装、そして特徴ある化粧など、歌舞伎は海外からの旅行者にも人気です。

□ 花道というのは、客席を通って舞台へと続く廊下のことです。

□ 三味線は日本の伝統的な弦楽器です。

□ 三味線は、日本の三弦リュートのようなものです。

□ 三味線は日本の伝統的な楽器で、弦を弾いて演奏します。

□ 三味線は日本の伝統的な弦楽器で、歌舞伎のほか、さまざまな伝統的行事などで使われます。

□ 歌舞伎の歴史は17世紀初期まで遡ることができます。

□ 歌舞伎は最初、京都で上演され、すぐに江戸に広がっていきました。

□ 歌舞伎の始まった17世紀初期は、女性だけが踊るものでした。

□ 本来、歌舞伎は女性が演じるものでしたが、幕府が性的な挑発になるということで、女性が演じることを禁止しました。

□ 幕府が、女性が演じる歌舞伎を禁じると、男性が男役、女役の両方を演じるようになりました。

□ 男性が女役を演じるという点で、歌舞伎はユニークな演劇といわれています。

□ 歌舞伎では、女性を演じる男性俳優を女形といいます。

□ 江戸時代、歌舞伎は舞台芸術として発展しました。

□ 江戸時代、舞台演劇として発展した歌舞伎は、江戸の人にも大阪の人にも喜ばれました。

安政５年（1858）の市村座の様子
（歌川豊国画）

The exotic dances, music, costumes, and distinctive makeup make *kabuki* popular with international visitors.

A *hanamichi* is an elevated runway extending through the audience's seats to the stage.

A *shamisen* is a traditional Japanese stringed instrument.

A *shamisen* is a three-stringed Japanese lute.

The *shamisen* is a traditional Japanese stringed instrument played by plucking the strings.

The *shamisen* is a traditional Japanese stringed instrument used in *kabuki* as well as in various other traditional events.

Kabuki's history can be traced back to the early seventeenth century.

Kabuki was first performed in Kyoto and soon spread to Edo, or modern-day Tokyo.

In the early 17th century, when *kabuki* began, only women danced.

Originally, *kabuki* was performed by women, but the shogunate banned women from performing it on the grounds that it would be sexually provocative.

When the shogunate banned women from performing *kabuki*, men began to play both male and female roles.

Kabuki is said to be unique in that men play female roles.

In *kabuki*, the male actors who play female roles are called *onnagata*.

During the Edo period, *kabuki* developed as a performing art.

During the Edo period, *kabuki* developed as a performing art and was appreciated by both the people of Edo and Osaka.

写楽による役者絵

□大阪や京都で発展した歌舞伎を上方歌舞伎といいます。

□歌舞伎で演じられる有名な演目の多くは、日本の古典を題材にしたものです。

□江戸時代、歌舞伎の人気役者を宣伝するために描かれたのが浮世絵です。

□東京で歌舞伎が行われるのは、主に国立劇場か歌舞伎座です。

□どちらの劇場でも、英語の翻訳付きで歌舞伎を楽しむことができます。

文楽

□文楽は日本の伝統的な人形劇です。

□文楽は人形浄瑠璃ともいいます。

□文楽は、17世紀の後半に竹本義太夫が大阪で劇場を始めたことで、人気が出ました。

□17世紀後半、近松門左衛門の作品を上演したことで、文楽は有名になりました。

□近松門左衛門は文楽のために物語を書いた脚本家です。

□文楽は大阪で始まり、歌舞伎にも大きな影響を与えました。

□文楽は歌舞伎の人形版のようなものです。

□文楽では、三味線の伴奏で物語が語られ、吟じられます。

□文楽で行われる語りを浄瑠璃といいます。

□浄瑠璃は文楽で行われる語りで、三味線の伴奏がつきます。

Kabuki developed in Osaka and Kyoto is called *Kamigata kabuki.*

Many of the famous plays performed in *kabuki* are based on Japanese classics.

During the Edo period, *ukiyo-e* woodblock prints were painted to advertise popular *kabuki* actors.

Kabuki is performed in Tokyo, mainly at the National Theater or the Kabuki-za Theater.

At either theater, you can enjoy *kabuki* performances with English translations.

Bunraku **(Puppet Theater)**

Bunraku is the traditional Japanese puppet theater of Japan.

Bunraku is also called *ningyo joruri.*

Bunraku became popular in the late 17th century when Takemoto Gidayu started a theater in Osaka.

In the late 17th century, *bunraku* became famous for its productions of works by Chikamatsu Monzaemon.

Chikamatsu Monzaemon was a playwright who wrote stories for *bunraku.*

Bunraku began in Osaka and had a great influence on *kabuki.*

Bunraku is like a puppet version of *kabuki* theater.

In *bunraku*, the story is spoken and chanted with the accompaniment of *shamisen.*

The chant done in *bunraku* is called *joruri.*

Joruri is the chant performed in *bunraku* with the accompaniment of *shamisen.*

能

□ 能は日本の古典芸能の一つです。

□ 能は日本の古典的な演劇で、13 ～ 14世紀に発展しました。

□ 能は日本の舞台演劇の中でも最もよく知られているものの一つです。

□ 能は猿楽から発展した歌舞劇で、踊りと劇の要素が含まれています。

□ 能は観阿弥が創始し、14世紀に息子の世阿弥が確立しました。

□ 能は観阿弥・世阿弥親子によって洗練された舞台芸術になりました。

□ 能役者の動きはとてもゆっくりしています。

□ 能はそのミニマリズムゆえに、洗練されていると言われています。

□ 能の主役は仕手と呼ばれ、助け役を脇といいます。

□ 能の舞台には、数人の役者しか上がらず、仕手と呼ばれる1人の役者が演じ、謡い、踊ります。

□ 能は男性の役者で演じられます。

□ 能の役者は、面を着けて演じます。

□ 能面は、能の役者が顔につけるマスクのことです。

□ 能の役者は面をつけ、面の角度による光や影を利用して、様々な顔の表情を作り出します。

□ 能の世界では、役者がゆっくりとした最小限の動きをしながら、能面で表情を創り出すことで、神秘的でかつ深淵な世界を描きます。

Noh (Classical Japanese dance-drama)

Noh is one of Japan's classical performing arts.

Noh is a classical Japanese theater form that developed in the 13th and 14th centuries.

Noh is one of the best-known Japanese performing arts.

Noh is a song-and-dance drama that evolved from *sarugaku*, a form of popular theater, and includes elements of dance and drama.

Noh was originated by Kan'ami and established by his son Zeami in the 14th century.

The father and son, Kan'ami and Zeami, refined Noh into a performing art.

The movements of noh actors are very slow.

Noh is said to be sophisticated because of its minimalism.

The main actor in a noh drama is called the *shite*. Supporting roles are called *waki*.

In noh theater, there are only a few actors, and an actor called a *shite* acts, chants, and dances.

Noh is performed by male actors.

Noh actors wear masks.

Noh masks are masks that noh actors wear on their faces.

Noh actors wear masks to create various facial expressions by using the light and shadows cast by the angles of the masks.

In the world of noh, actors create a profound and mysterious atmosphere with their slow, minimized actions and the expressions created with the masks they wear.

□ 夢幻能とは、15世紀に世阿弥が完成した劇で、亡霊や神などが物語を語ります。

□ 薪能は、薪をたいて野外で行う能のことです。

□ 囃しとは、能舞台の伴奏のことです。もともとは、笛と3種の太鼓で伴奏しました。

□ 鼓は日本古来の打楽器です。小さな鼓は、肩にのせて右手で打ちます。

□ 大鼓は座っている膝の上にのせて演奏します。

□ 太鼓は日本式のドラムのことで、能では小さい太鼓が使われます。

□ 謡は、登場人物の台詞に節をつけた歌のことで、もともとは8人で歌っていました。

狂言

□ 狂言は能楽師が演じる滑稽劇です。

□ 時には狂言が独立して演じられることもありました。この場合は、本狂言と呼ばれました。

□ 狂言は能と源流は同じです。

□ 能と違って、ほとんどの狂言は面を着けることはありません。

□ 狂言の主役はシテと呼ばれ、脇役をアドといいます。

□ 狂言は中世の庶民の日常生活を題材にした、台詞が中心の喜劇です。

狂言の舞台

Mugen Noh (Dreamlike Noh) are plays written by Zeami in the 15th century, in which ghosts and deities tell stories.

Takigi-noh is noh that is enjoyed outside with torches.

Hayashi is the music played upstage in noh performances. Ordinarily, a flute and three kinds of drums provide the accompaniment.

The *tsuzumi* is an ancient Japanese percussion instrument. The small *tsuzumi* is placed on the shoulder and struck with the right hand.

The *taiko* drum is played on the seated person's lap.

Taiko are Japanese drums, and small *taiko* are used in noh.

The chant is a song with verses added to the characters' lines, and was originally sung by eight people.

Kyogen **(Comic Theater)**

Kyogen is a comic play performed by a noh actor.

Sometimes *kyogen* was performed independently. In this case, it was called *hon kyogen*.

Kyogen has the same origin as noh.

Unlike noh, almost all *kyogen* is performed without masks.

In *kyogen*, the main role is called the *shite*, and supporting roles are called *ado*.

Kyogen is a comic drama based on the daily life of common people in the Middle Ages, and is mainly composed of dialogues.

着物

□ 着物は日本の伝統的な衣装です。

□ 着物は日本の伝統的な衣装で、男性、女性ともに着ます。

□ 女性が着る着物は色鮮やかです。

□ 着物は、洋服と区別して和服と呼ばれます。

□ 着物は衣服というだけでなく、素晴らしい芸術でもあります。

□ 着物は一般的には高いものです。

□ 色鮮やかで、一流の染め技術が施された着物は、とても高価です。

□ 着物を寝間着と思っている人もいますが、それは間違いです。

□ 外国人用に、寝間着として着物もどきのものを販売する土産物屋も多いです。

□ 着物用の織物をつくるには、熟練した職人技が必要です。

□ 着物を仕立てるには、先代から受け継がれる熟練の技が必要です。

□ 京都や金沢でつくられる高級な着物の中に、友禅と呼ばれるものがあります。

□ 友禅は高級な着物で、京都や金沢でつくられます。

□ 友禅（染め）は、1年がかりで布に絵付けや染めを施します。

□ 着物を着るときは、腰のところに帯を巻いて、背中で結びます。

Kimono

Kimonos are a type of traditional Japanese clothing.

Kimonos are a type of traditional Japanese clothing for both males and females.

Kimonos worn by women are brightly colored.

Kimonos are often called *wafuku* to distinguish Japanese clothing from Western clothes, which is called *yofuku* in Japanese.

Kimonos are not only clothing but exquisite works of art as well.

Kimonos are generally expensive.

Kimonos, particularly the ones with colorful designs and high-quality dye, are quite expensive.

Some may think that kimonos are a type of housecoat, but it is not true.

Many souvenir shops sell fake kimonos as housecoats for foreign visitors.

The textile work involved in making kimonos requires skilled artisanship.

Tailoring a kimono requires skilled craftsmanship passed down from previous generations.

Some of the highest-quality kimonos produced in Kyoto and Kanazawa are called *yuzen*.

Yuzen are the highest-quality kimonos, and they are produced in Kyoto and Kanazawa.

Yuzen involves a yearlong process for the designing and dyeing of the fabric.

When wearing a kimono, an *obi*, or sash, is wrapped around the waist and tied behind the back.

□ 帯を結ぶには技術が必要で、自分でやるのはかなり大変です。

□ 帯を自分で結ぶのはかなり大変で､着物を着る人はたいてい誰かに助けてもらいます。

□ 振り袖は、未婚女性が着る袖の長い着物のことです。

□ 未婚女性は、色鮮やかで、袖の長い振り袖を着ます。

□ 既婚女性は、袖の短い留袖という着物を着ます。

□ 既婚女性は、落ち着いた色の袖の短い留袖を着ます。

□ 浴衣は着物の一種で、夏の夜に着ます。

□ 浴衣はもともとは夜に着る室内着でしたが､外を散歩するときなどにも着られるようになりました。

□ 最近では、花火やお祭りでも浴衣を着る人がいます。

□ 日本の伝統的な宿である旅館では、浴衣を借りて温泉に行くことができます。

□ 浴衣はふだん着なので、高級なホテルのロビーではふさわしくありません。

□ 日本人は日常生活では洋服を着ていますが、結婚式、葬儀、卒業式など特別な場合に着物を着ます。

Tying the sash requires skill, and it is quite difficult to do by yourself.

It is quite difficult to tie the sash by yourself, and kimono wearers usually have someone help them.

A *furisode* is a type of kimono with long sleeves worn by girls before they are married.

Unmarried women wear brightly colored *furisode* with long sleeves.

A *tomesode* is a type of kimono with shorter sleeves for married women.

Once a woman marries, she wears a *tomesode*, a less colorful kimono with shorter sleeves.

A *yukata* is a type of kimono and is worn on summer evenings.

Originally, *yukata* were worn indoors at night, but they are now also worn when taking a walk outside.

These days, people wear *yukata* when they are watching fireworks or attending festivals.

In a *ryokan*, or traditional Japanese inn, people can borrow *yukata* to visit hot springs.

Wearing a *yukata* in the lobby of high-class hotels is not proper because they are considered to be informal attire.

Although Japanese people wear Western clothes in daily life, they wear kimonos for special occasions, such as weddings, funerals, graduation ceremonies, and so on.

茶道

□茶道は茶を点ててそれを振るまう日本の伝統的な儀式です。

□茶道は何世紀にもわたる歴史があり、そこには哲学的な概念が潜んでいます。

□茶道では、粉末にした抹茶が用いられます。

□普通の茶葉からつくられる緑茶に比べ、抹茶は濃厚な味がします。

□茶道は禅とともに発展し、16世紀後半に千利休という人によって確立されました。

□茶道が16世紀後半に広まると、人々は洗練されたしきたりで振るまわれる一杯のお茶に心を和ませました。

□茶道は単に茶を飲むだけではありません。繊細で美しい雰囲気も魅力です。

□茶道では、茶を振るまう茶碗を愛でることも重要です。

□茶室と呼ばれる茶を点てる部屋には、生け花や掛け軸が飾られ、洗練された雰囲気を醸し出しています。

高台寺の遺芳庵

□茶道は大切な客をもてなすために、洗練された雰囲気を作り出す芸術です。

□茶道にはさまざまな作法があります。茶室への入り方、挨拶の仕方、お菓子の食べ方、茶の飲み方などを覚える必要があります。

□複雑な作法は、日本人でもよく知りません。大切なのは、リラックスしてその雰囲気や伝統を楽しむことです。

生け花

□生け花は日本の伝統的なフラワーアレンジメントのことです。

Tea Ceremony

The tea ceremony is a traditional Japanese ritual in which tea is prepared and served.

The tea ceremony has centuries of history and many philosophical concepts behind it.

The tea served at tea ceremonies is *matcha*, which is made from powdered tea.

Matcha has a stronger taste than regular green tea brewed from ordinary tea leaves.

The tea ceremony developed along with Zen and was established in the late 16th century by a man named Sen no Rikyu.

As the tea ceremony spread in the late 16th century, people were comforted by a cup of tea served according to a refined ritual.

The tea ceremony is not only about drinking tea. It is also about the delicate and beautiful atmosphere.

In the tea ceremony, it is also important to appreciate the bowl in which the tea is served.

In a tea room called a *chashitsu*, there is a flower arrangement called an ikebana and a hanging scroll to create a refined atmosphere.

The tea ceremony is the art of creating a refined atmosphere for entertaining important guests.

In the tea ceremony, guests have to follow complex procedures, for example, when they enter a tea room, greet, eat a confection, and drink tea.

Even Japanese people aren't familiar with the intricate details of the tea ceremony. What's truly important is to relax and savor the atmosphere and tradition.

Ikebana

Ikebana is the art of traditional Japanese flower arrangement.

□ 生け花のことを華道ともいい、この伝統的な日本のフラワーアレンジメントは、室町時代に発展しました。

□ 明治時代以降、生け花のコンセプトは、西洋のフラワーアレンジメントにも影響を与えました。

□ 生け花が空間の芸術と言われるのは、空間と花のラインを組み合わせるものだからです。

□ 池坊は、日本最大の華道の流派です。

□ 池坊専慶は室町時代の僧で、池坊流の華道の基礎をつくりました。

短歌・俳句

□ 短歌は日本の伝統的な詩で、5－7－5－7－7の五句体です。

□ 最初の3句を上の句、あとの2句を下の句といいます。

□ 短歌は古代よりつくられています。

□ 昔は感情や思いを伝えるために短歌を交換しました。

□ 辞世とは、死ぬ前につくられる短歌のことです。

□ 俳句は、短歌の上の句から生まれました。俳句は5－7－5の3句からなります。

□ 俳句は海外にも紹介され、世界中で楽しまれています。

□ 川柳は風刺や皮肉を盛り込んだ詩で、俳句と同じ形式です。江戸時代に流行しました。

□ 狂歌は風刺や皮肉を盛り込んだ詩で、短歌と同じ形式です。江戸時代に流行しました。

Ikebana is also called *kado*, or flower arrangement, and this traditional Japanese floral arrangement art developed during the Muromachi period.

The concept of Ikebana has had an influence on Western flower arrangement since the Meiji period.

Ikebana can be said to be a spatial art because the arrangement is created based on the relationship between space and the flowers' line.

Ikenobo is the largest school of flower arrangement in Japan.

Senkei Ikenobo was a Muromachi period monk who laid the foundation for the Ikenobo school of flower arrangement.

Tanka (Short Poems) and Haiku

A *tanka* is a traditional Japanese poem consisting of five verses based on lines of 5-7-5-7-7 syllables.

The first three verses of *tanka* are called a *kaminoku*, and the latter two verses are called a *shimonoku*.

Tanka have been written since ancient times.

People used to exchange *tanka* to communicate their feelings and thoughts.

A *jisei* is a *tanka* that is written just before someone's death.

The haiku was born from *tanka*'s *kaminoku*. The haiku consists of three parts based on the verses of 5-7-5 syllables.

Haiku has been introduced to and enjoyed around the world.

Senryu is a poem that incorporates satire and irony and is in the same form as haiku. It became popular during the Edo period.

Kyoka are iconic, satirized verses with the same form as *tanka*. They were popular in the Edo period.

現代文化・風潮

伝統の日本だけでなく、今の日本を紹介します。マンガ・アニメ、オタク文化から、コスプレまで、新しい日本の情報を英語で話してみましょう。

マンガ・アニメ

□ マンガとは、日本のコミックまたはグラフィックノベルのことです。

□ マンガは、日本のポップカルチャーの中でも最もよく知られています。

□ 今ではマンガという言葉は、世界中で知られています。

□ 50年代、60年代にはマンガ家が素晴らしい話を作り出し、マンガ雑誌を出版する出版社にとっては稼ぎ頭となりました。

□ マンガはずっと長いこと人気があったので、あらゆる世代の日本の人々に読まれ、楽しまれています。

□ 出版社は、マンガを取り入れたハウツー本、ノンフィクション本、さらには若者・大人向けに教育的な本を出版することもあります。

□ 京都には日本初のマンガミュージアムがあり、貴重な資料や展示を見たり、国内外で人気の名作を読んだりすることができます。

□ マンガだけでなくアニメも同様、ビジュアルはコンピューターで制作され、この形式は日本から世界へと広がっていきました。

□ 日本のアニメは、ジャンルの幅広さや物語の世界観、作画の質の高さから、海外でも絶大な人気を誇っています。

□ アニメの主題歌やBGMに使用された日本の楽曲も、海外での人気が高まっています。

Track 13

Manga and Anime

Manga is a Japanese comic or graphic novel.

Manga are one of the best-known forms of Japanese pop culture.

Today, the word manga is known all over the world.

In the 50s and 60s, manga artists created fantastic stories, and the manga magazines put out by major publishers were huge moneymakers.

Manga have been loved for so long that now they are read and enjoyed by all generations in Japan.

Sometimes publishers even make manga versions of how-to books, nonfiction, and even educational content for both young people and adults.

Kyoto is home to Japan's first Manga Museum, where you can see valuable materials and exhibits, and read popular masterpieces from Japan and abroad.

Not only in manga but in anime as well, visual art is created by computer, and these art forms have spread from Japan to the rest of the world.

Japanese anime is immensely popular overseas due to the wide range of genres, the worldview of the stories, and the quality of the artwork.

Japanese songs used as theme songs and background music for anime are also becoming increasingly popular overseas.

オタク文化

□ オタク文化は、アニメ、SF、マンガといった日本のポップカルチャーや若者のライフスタイルの象徴です。

□ オタクとは、アニメやゲームなど特定の分野に興味を持つ人たちのことです。

□ オタク文化は、今では世界中に広まっています。

□ オタクと並んで海外に紹介された「かわいい」は、英語で「キュート」や「チャーミング」と言います。

□ 多くの日本人は、何か愛らしいものを見ると「かわいい」と言います。

□ 秋葉原や池袋は、東京都内のオタク文化の中心地です。

□ 秋葉原や池袋には、オタク文化の象徴的な品やコスチュームを売る店がたくさんあります。

コスプレ

□ 今ではコスプレは世界中で認知されています。コスチュームとプレイの造語です。

□ コスプレとは、アニメ、ゲーム、マンガなどのキャラクターを真似て、コスチュームを着て、化粧をしたりすることです。

□ コスプレを趣味や仕事にしている人のことを「コスプレイヤー」と呼びます。

□ 日本のアニメ、マンガ、コンピューターゲームが世界中の若者に人気があるため、日本発のコスプレも多くの国に広まっています。

□ メイドカフェでは、かわいいメイドのコスチュームを着た少女が、コーヒーや飲み物を出してくれます。

Otaku Culture

Otaku culture represents Japanese pop culture including anime, science fiction, and manga as well as the lifestyles of young people.

Otaku are people who are interested in a particular field, such as anime or video games.

Otaku culture has now spread throughout the world.

The concept of *kawaii* that was introduced overseas alongside *otaku* is referred to as "cute" or "charming" in English.

Many Japanese people say, "*kawaii*" when they see something adorable.

Akihabara and Ikebukuro are the center of *otaku* culture in Tokyo.

Akihabara and Ikebukuro are home to many stores selling items and costumes that are symbolic of *otaku* culture.

Cosplay

Now cosplay is a globally recognized word. It is a combination of "costume" and "play."

Cosplay is the act of wearing costumes and makeup to imitate characters from anime, video games, manga, etc.

People who enjoy cosplay as a hobby or job are called "cosplayers."

Because Japanese anime, manga, and computer games are popular among young people around the world, cosplay started in Japan has also spread to many countries.

At maid cafes, girls in cute maid costumes serve coffee and drinks.

J- ポップ・演歌

□ 第二次世界大戦後、多くのポップミュージックが日本に紹介され、日本にある昔からの音楽と結びつきました。

□ Ｊポップは、ジャパニーズ・ポップ・ミュージックの略で、日本だけでなく、多くの国々でも売られています。

□ Ｊポップを通して、日本の最新のポップミュージックの詩やリズムが楽しまれています。

□ 演歌は、大衆音楽のジャンルのひとつで、日本古来の民謡の影響があります。

□ 演歌で歌われるのは、愛、情念、日本の心などです。

□ 世界的に有名なＫポップと言われる韓国のポップミュージックも、日本人の間でとても人気があります。

コンビニ文化

□ コンビニは、英語の"コンビニエンスストアconvenience store"の略称です。「便利な店」という意味です。

□ コンビニなしには、日本の都会での生活は成り立ちません。

□ 日本のコンビニでは、24時間いつでもどこのお店に行っても、同じような商品・サービスを得ることができます。

□ 日本全国にコンビニは5万5000軒以上あります。

□ コンビニで、公共料金を払ったり、オンラインで注文した本を受け取ったり、荷物を送ったりすることができます。

□ もし出張先で下着や靴下が足りなくなったら、コンビニに行って買うことができます。

J-Pop (Japanese Pop) and *Enka* (Sentimental Ballads)

After World War II, many kinds of popular music were introduced to Japan and combined with Japanese traditional popular music.

J-pop, short for Japanese pop music, is sold not only in Japan but also in many other countries.

Through J-pop, people can enjoy the new beats and original lyrics of Japan's newest form of popular music.

Enka is a genre of Japanese popular music with a traditional folk flavor.

The songs sung in *enka* are about love, emotion, and the Japanese spirit.

The world-famous Korean pop music known as K-pop is also very popular among Japanese people.

Convenience Store Culture

Konbini is a foreign loan word from the English "convenience store" and means "convenient store."

Life in urban Japan would not be possible without convenience stores.

Convenience stores in Japan offer the same products and services 24 hours a day, 7 days a week, no matter where you go.

There are more than 55,000 convenience stores throughout Japan.

At a convenience store, you can pay utility bills, pick up books you ordered online, or send packages.

If you run out of underwear or socks on a business trip, you can go to a convenience store to buy them.

携帯文化

□ 多くの日本人が、雑誌や新聞に代わり、デジタルコンテンツから情報を得ています。

□ 携帯電話とインターネットの普及によって、日本人のライフスタイルと文化は変わりました。

□ 絵文字は、e メールやスマホでメッセージを送るときに使います。

□ 犯罪などの違法行為をするウェブサイトを、闇サイトと呼びます。

□ 犯罪から子どもを守るために、スマホのGPS機能が使われることもあります。

Mobile Culture

Many Japanese people are getting their information from digital content instead of magazines and newspapers.

Cell phones and the internet have changed the lifestyle and culture of the Japanese people.

Emoji are used to send messages via e-mail and smartphones.

Websites that commit crimes and other illegal activities are called dark sites.

GPS functions on smartphones are sometimes used to protect children from crime.

スポーツ

古来より行われてきた伝統ある相撲から、柔道、空手、剣道、合気道まで日本の武道を紹介します。

相撲

□ 相撲とは、日本の伝統的なレスリングのことです。

□ 相撲の起源は、古代まで遡ることができます。

□ 相撲は神々を崇拝するための特別な取組として発展しました。

□ 歴史的に、相撲は神道と深い関係があります。

□ 相撲の取組は、神々への感謝を表すために行われました。

□ 土俵は力士が相撲を取る特別なリングのことです。

□ 相撲取りは、神聖な場所とされる土俵というリングで取り組みを行います。

□ 今では職業としての相撲の興行は、日本相撲協会が主催しています。

□ 今では相撲の興行は、日本相撲協会が主催しており、2ヵ月ごとに行われます。

□ 公式な相撲の取組は2ヵ月ごと、15日間にわたって行われます。

□ 公式な相撲の取組では、最も多くの取り組みに勝った力士が、優勝となります。

□ 相撲の番付の最上位は横綱です。番付とは力士のランクを表す順位表のことです。

Track 14

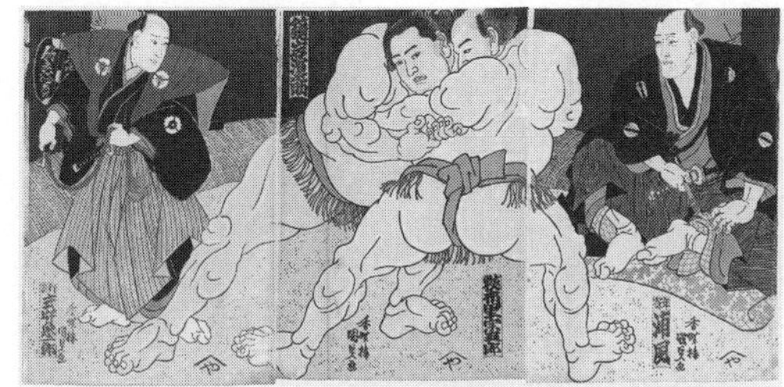

1860 年代、歌川国貞による相撲絵

Sumo Wrestling

Sumo is traditional Japanese wrestling.

Sumo's origin can be traced back to ancient times.

Sumo developed as a special type of wrestling performed to worship gods and goddesses.

Historically, sumo has close ties with Shinto.

Sumo matches were held to express gratitude to the gods.

A *dohyo* is a special ring in which wrestlers fight.

Sumo wrestlers fight in rings called *dohyo*, which are considered to be sacred.

Nowadays, sumo as a profession is organized by the Japan Sumo Association.

Sumo tournaments are now organized by the Japan Sumo Association and are held every two months.

Official sumo competitions are held every two months, and these continue for 15 days.

In official sumo competitions, the wrestler who wins the most bouts is the champion.

The *yokozuna* are the highest-ranked wrestlers in the sumo ranks. A *banzuke* is a ranking chart that shows the ranks of the wrestlers.

□力士は成績によってランク付けされており、最も高いのが横綱です。

□現代のスポーツとしての相撲にも、古来から続く伝統様式が多く残っています。

□相撲取りの独特の髪型は、封建時代から変わっていません。

□相撲を取る際、力士たちはほぼ裸同然です。

□力士は、どこにも武器を隠していないことを証明するために、ほぼ裸同然で相撲を取ります。

□相撲を取るとき、力士はまわしと呼ばれるふんどしのようなものしか身に着けません。

□取り組みの前、力士は多くの儀式に従わなければなりません。

□古代まで遡れる相撲の儀式に、外国人は引きつけられます。

□人々は、ほかでは見られない儀式や、激しい取組に魅了されます。

□相撲はスポーツとしてだけでなく、美的に優れた伝統としても楽しまれています。

□土俵に上がる前、力士は口をすすぎます。

□土俵の上で、力士は塩をまき、邪悪なものを取り払います。

□土俵上で、力士は四股を踏みますが、これは病気や不幸などの悪い気を地下に押し込めるためです。

□土俵上で、力士はしゃがんで、神への挨拶としてパンと両手をたたきます。

□力士が所属する個別の組織を部屋と呼び、親方と呼ばれる主が力士の面倒を見ます。

□力士は朝食の前に、それぞれの部屋の土俵で激しい稽古を行います。

Wrestlers are ranked according to their performance, with *yokozuna* being the highest.

Although sumo is a modern sport, many traditional aspects from ancient times remain.

The unique hairstyle of sumo wrestlers has not changed since the feudal era.

Wrestlers are almost naked when they compete.

Wrestlers compete almost naked to prove that they have no weapons hidden anywhere.

When wrestling, wrestlers wear only a *mawashi*, a loincloth-like garment.

Before the bout, wrestlers must follow a number of rituals.

Foreigners are drawn to the rituals of sumo, which date back to ancient times.

People are fascinated by the unique rituals and the intensity of the matches.

Sumo is enjoyed not only as a sport, but also as an aesthetically pleasing tradition.

Before stepping into the ring, a wrestler rinses his mouth.

Inside the ring, sumo wrestlers throw salt to ward off evil spirits.

In the ring, sumo wrestlers stamp their feet to stomp evil spirits that cause illness and misfortune into the ground.

In the ring, wrestlers squat and clap their hands in greeting to the gods.

The individual organization to which a wrestler belongs is called a stable, and the master, called an *oyakata*, takes care of the wrestlers.

Before breakfast, wrestlers practice hard in the rings of their respective stables.

□ 国技館は相撲の本拠地で、東京の両国にあります。

□ 東京の両国近辺には50ほどの相撲部屋があります。

□ 相撲は伝統的なスポーツですが、近年はモンゴルやヨーロッパからも多くの外国人力士が日本にやって来て、競技に参加しています。

野球

□ 野球は、サッカーや相撲と並び、日本で最も人気のあるスポーツのひとつです。

□ 学校や町にある地元の野球チームに多くの子どもたちが参加しています。

□ 1年に2度、春と夏には大阪近くの甲子園で、全国的な高校野球の大会が行われます。

□ 夏の全国高等学校野球選手権大会では、各県で優勝したチームの熱烈な応援団が集まり、自分たちの代表を応援します。まるでお祭りのような雰囲気です。

□ 才能を見出された選手は、早い段階からプロ野球への道が開かれます。

□ 野球が日本に紹介されたのは1872年のことです。

□ 野球は1872年に日本に紹介され、1920年にはプロ野球リーグが発足しました。

□ 日本にはプロ野球の球団が12あります。

□ 現在日本にはセ・リーグとパ・リーグの2つのリーグがあります。

□ アメリカのメジャーリーグにスカウトされるプロ選手も年々増えています。

The Kokugikan is the home of sumo and is located in Ryogoku, Tokyo.

There are about 50 sumo stables in the Ryogoku area of Tokyo.

Sumo is a traditional sport, but in recent years, many foreign wrestlers from Mongolia and Europe have come to Japan to compete.

Baseball

Baseball is one of the most popular sports in Japan, together with soccer and sumo.

Many children participate in local baseball teams in their schools and towns.

Twice a year, in the spring and summer, a National High School Baseball Championship is held at the Koshien Stadium near Osaka.

At the national high school baseball championships in summer, enthusiastic supporters of the winning teams in each prefecture gather to cheer on their representatives. The atmosphere is like a festival.

A path to the major leagues is opened for young athletes who show talent.

Baseball was introduced to Japan in 1872.

Baseball was introduced to Japan in 1872, and a professional baseball league was established in 1920.

There are 12 professional baseball teams in Japan.

There are currently two leagues in Japan: the Central League and the Pacific League.

The number of professional players scouted by Major League Baseball in the US is increasing every year.

サッカー

□野球と同じように、日本ではサッカーもさかんです。

□アジアでは、日本の強敵は韓国です。

□2002年のワールドカップは日本と韓国の共催でした。

□ Ｊリーグは日本のプロサッカーリーグで、1991年に発足しました。

□多くの日本人サッカー選手が、日本以外の国でプレーしています。

柔道

□柔道は1882年に嘉納治五郎が創始した武道です。

□柔道は世界中に広まり、オリンピック競技になっています。

□柔道は日本の武道で、国を超え広がっています。

□柔道は、古くは柔術と呼ばれた武道から派生したものです。

□柔道の技は、投技、固技、当身技があります。

□柔道の礼は、相手への敬意です。そのため対戦の前と後には互いにお辞儀をします。

□柔道の技は、攻撃をしかけずに相手の力を利用して勝つことです。柔は剛を制すと言われています。

Soccer

Like baseball, soccer is also popular in Japan.

In Asia, Japan's strongest rival is South Korea.

The 2002 World Cup was cohosted by Japan and Korea.

The J-League, Japan's professional soccer league, was established in 1991.

Many Japanese soccer players play in countries other than Japan.

Judo

Judo is a martial art founded by Jigoro Kano in 1882.

Judo has spread throughout the world and has become an Olympic sport.

Judo is a Japanese martial art that has spread internationally.

Judo is derived from the ancient martial art called *jujutsu*.

Judo's fighting techniques consist of throwing, grappling, and striking techniques.

Part of judo's etiquette is to respect one's opponent. For this reason, practitioners have to bow to each other before and after a match.

Judo uses technique to utilize the opponent's power against him or her without initiating aggressive attacks to win. It says that softness overcomes hardness.

空手

□空手は沖縄発祥の武道です。

□空手はカンフーとは違います。沖縄生まれの武道で、古い中国の拳法を取り入れながら発展したものです。

□空手は素手で敵を倒す武道です。

□空手は自分の体を鍛え、それを武器とする武道です。

□空手は腕、手、足、頭を武器のように使う武道です。

□空手は防御のためのもので、攻撃されたときだけ戦います。

□空手のユニークな点は、そのスピードにあります。空手家は瞬時にすべての力を集中させ、防御から攻撃に移ります。

□柔道のように、今では空手も世界に広まっています。

□空手では、師は弟子に対戦のパターンとして多くの型を学ばせます。

合気道

□合気道は日本の武道の一つで、空手同様、素手で相手を制します。

□合気道は日本の武道で、柔道のもとである柔術から発祥しました。

□合気道がユニークな武道と言われるのは、名人が相手の力を瞬時に、大した動きもなく奪うことができるからです。

□合気道は、瞬く間に相手の力を使って倒します。

□合気道は、反撃がうまくいくと、瞬時に相手を動けなくします。

Karate

Karate is a martial art that originated in Okinawa.

Karate is different from Kung Fu. It is an Okinawan-born martial art that developed while incorporating old Chinese kung-fu techniques.

Karate is a martial art in which one defeats the enemy with one's bare hands.

Karate is a martial art in which practitioners train their body to become a weapon.

Karate is a martial art that uses the arms, hands, legs, and the head as its weapons.

Karate is a defensive art, and participants fight only when attacked.

One unique aspect of karate is its speed. Karate practitioners focus all their power instantly and move from defense to attack.

Like judo, karate has now spread throughout the world.

In karate, the master has his apprentice learn many *kata*, or forms, which represent fighting patterns.

Aikido

Aikido is a Japanese martial art that, like karate, uses bare hands to dominate an opponent.

Aikido is a Japanese martial art that originated from *jujutsu*, from which judo is derived.

Aikido is considered a unique martial art because a master can take away his opponent's power instantly and without much movement.

Aikido uses the power of the opponent to defeat him in the blink of an eye.

Aikido instantly immobilizes the opponent when a counterattack is successful.

剣道

□剣道は日本の武道の一つです。

□日本の剣術の技は、内乱が続いた16世紀頃に発展しました。

□江戸時代、侍は道場と呼ばれる稽古場で剣の技を磨きました。

□江戸時代、独自の剣術の技を作り上げた名人がたくさんいました。

□近代の剣道は、竹刀と防具を使って試合をします。

□剣道では、面、胴、小手を打つことでポイントが入ります。首の前側を突くことでもポイントが入ります。

□中学校では、武道の授業として柔道と剣道を採用しているところが多いです。

Kendo

Kendo is one of the Japanese martial arts.

The art of Japanese swordsmanship developed around the 16th century during a period of civil war.

During the Edo period, samurai honed their swordsmanship skills in training halls called *dojo*.

During the Edo period, there were many masters who created their own unique swordsmanship techniques.

In modern kendo, matches are held with *shinai* (bamboo swords) and protective gear.

In kendo, points are awarded for striking the face, body, and forearm. Points are also awarded for thrusting at the front of the neck.

Many junior high schools offer classes in judo and kendo to teach martial arts.

\ちょこっと/

知っておきたい日本紹介のコツ④

● 相手にサービスや援助を提供するとき

もし、外国のお客さんに対して情報を提供しなければならない立場にあった場合、相手に対して「How can I help you?（何かお役に立てることがありますか？）」と切り出すのが一般的です。もちろん、行き先に迷っている人に「Can I help you?（どうしましたか？）」とカジュアルに声をかけることも良いことです。こうした切り出すためのフレーズはいつも心に留めておきたいものですね。

● 意外と不親切な日本の公共機関

よく新幹線や飛行機などで英語のアナウンスを耳にします。しかし、ほとんどは定型文のアナウンスだけで、例えば列車の到着が遅れるなどといったハプニングが起こると、車掌さんが日本語でアナウンスするのみで、英語でのアナウンスはほとんど聞くことがありません。

特に日本は地震や津波、大雨などの災害が多く、慣れない土地で初めて経験する災害に驚き、不安を抱く外国人の方々も多くいることでしょう。日本の事情を紹介・説明するフレーズに加えて、こうした緊急時の英語を習得しておくことも必要ではないでしょうか。「Train will be late due to the earthquake in Shizuoka area.（静岡地域で発生した地震のために、列車は遅れるようです）」などといった簡単な表現をストックしておけると良いでしょう。

第5章

日本各地の説明

東京
京都
大阪
北海道
東北地方
関東地方
中部地方
近畿地方
中国地方
四国地方
九州地方

東京

日本の首都である東京には、毎年多くの外国人旅行者が訪れます。東京の概要、交通、歴史、江戸情緒、そして観光スポットについて英語で語ってみましょう。

東京の概要

□ 東京は日本の首都です。

□ 東京は日本の政治、経済、文化の中心です。

□ 東京は巨大な都市です。

□ 東京は巨大な都市で、一日では堪能できません。

□ 東京は人口が密集した都市です。

□ 東京は巨大で、人口が密集しています。

□ 東京都の人口は約1400万人です。

□ 現在、東京都には約1400万人が住んでいます。

□ 東京都には23区あります。

□ 東京23区には、約970万人が住んでいます。

□ 東京都と周辺地域をあわせ、首都圏といいます。

□ 首都圏は東京都のほかに、神奈川、埼玉、千葉県で構成されています。

□ 首都圏には、約3560万人が住んでいます。

Track 15

都庁

Tokyo Overview

Tokyo is the capital of Japan.

Tokyo is the political, economic, and cultural center of Japan.

Tokyo is a huge city.

Tokyo is a huge city and cannot be fully explored in a single day.

Tokyo is a densely populated city.

Tokyo is huge and densely populated.

The population of Tokyo is approximately 14 million.

Currently, there are 14 million people living in Tokyo.

Tokyo has 23 wards.

Approximately 9.7 million people live in the 23 wards of Tokyo.

Tokyo and its surrounding areas are collectively known as the Tokyo Metropolitan Area.

The Tokyo metropolitan area consists of Kanagawa, Saitama, and Chiba prefectures in addition to Tokyo.

Approximately 35.6 million people live in the Tokyo Metropolitan Area.

□ 現在、970万の人が東京23区に住んでいて、首都圏には3560万の人が住んでいます。

□ 首都圏は、世界のどの大都市圏よりも人口が多いです。

□ 日本のGDPのおよそ5分の1はここで生み出されています。

東京の交通

□ 東京では、電車と地下鉄を使うことをおすすめします。

□ 東京の電車と地下鉄のネットワークはとても効率的です。

□ 東京だけで50以上の電車と地下鉄が走っています。

□ 東京では、50以上の通勤電車、地下鉄が走っています。

□ 東京の新宿駅は毎日350万人以上の乗客が利用しています。

□ 東京の百貨店やショッピングセンターは、主要駅の上に直接建てられています。

□ 東京には、主要駅をつなぐ山手線という環状線があり、ほかの私鉄や地下鉄に乗り換えることができます。

□ 東京駅は新幹線の終着駅で、日本中から新幹線が到着します。

□ 東京駅は新幹線の終着駅で、ここから東京の各地へ向かう電車や地下鉄に乗り換えることができます。

東京駅

□ 羽田空港は、日本各地から東京へ来るときの空の玄関口です。

□ 羽田空港は、日本各地から東京へ来るときの空の玄関口であり、かつ国際空港でもあります。

□ 山手線の浜松町駅で、羽田空港行きのモノレールに乗り換えられます。

Currently, 9.7 million people live in the 23 wards of Tokyo, and 35.6 million people live in the Tokyo Metropolitan Area.

The Tokyo Metropolitan Area has more people than any other metropolitan area in the world.

Approximately one-fifth of Japan's GDP is generated there.

Transportation in Tokyo

In Tokyo, it is highly recommended that one use the train or subway.

Tokyo's train and subway network is very efficient.

There are more than 50 train lines and subways in Tokyo alone.

There are more than 50 commuter train lines and subways in Tokyo.

Shinjuku station in Tokyo is used by more than 3.5 million passengers every day.

Tokyo's department stores and shopping centers are built directly on top of major stations.

Tokyo has a loop line, the Yamanote Line, that connects major stations and allows for transfers to other private railways and subways.

Tokyo Station is the terminus for the Shinkansen bullet trains, which arrive from all over Japan.

Tokyo Station is the terminus for Shinkansen bullet trains, from which you can transfer to trains and subways heading to various parts of Tokyo.

Haneda is the air gateway to Tokyo from Japan's outlying cities.

Haneda Airport is the gateway to Tokyo from all over Japan and is also an international airport.

At Hamamatsucho Station on the Yamanote Line, you can transfer to the monorail to reach Haneda Airport.

□ 東京の主要駅は、東京、品川、渋谷、新宿、池袋、そして上野です。

東京の歴史

□ 東京とは、「東の都」の意味です。

□ 東京という名は、1869年まで都だった京都から、東に450キロの位置に移ったことからきています。

□ 東京の歴史は、江戸城が建てられた1457年に始まりました。

□ 1869年以前、東京は江戸と呼ばれていました。

□ 江戸は東京の旧称です。

□ 1603年から1868年の間、幕府は江戸にありました。

□ 江戸は幕府があったところです。

□ 1868年までは、幕府は江戸にあり、宮廷は京都にありました。

□ 1869年に天皇が京都から東京に移り、東京は日本の首都になりました。

□ 江戸城は、現在は天皇の住まいである皇居となり、東京の中心部に位置しています。

□ 現在の皇居である江戸城は、東京駅の近くにあります。

□ 18世紀の江戸は、日本国内だけでなく世界でも最も人口の密集した都市でした。

□ 20世紀、東京は二度、ひどい被害を受けました。

□ 東京は1923年の関東大震災という地震で大きな被害を受けました。

Major stations in Tokyo are Tokyo, Shinagawa, Shibuya, Shinjuku, Ikebukuro, and Ueno.

History of Tokyo

Tokyo means "Eastern capital."

The name "Tokyo" comes from its location 450 km east of Kyoto, which was the capital until 1869.

Tokyo's history began in 1457, when Edo Castle was built.

Prior to 1869, Tokyo was called Edo.

Edo is the former name of Tokyo.

From 1603 to 1868, the shogunate was located in Edo.

Edo was where the shogunate was located.

Until 1868, the shogunate was in Edo, and the emperor's court was in Kyoto.

In 1869, the Emperor moved from Kyoto to Tokyo, and Tokyo became the capital of Japan.

Edo Castle, now the Imperial Palace, the residence of the Emperor, is located in the center of Tokyo.

Edo Castle, which is now the Imperial Palace, is located near Tokyo Station.

In the 18th century, Edo was the most densely populated city not only in Japan but also in the world.

In the 20th century, Tokyo was severely damaged two times.

Tokyo was severely damaged by the Great Kanto Earthquake of 1923.

□東京は第二次世界大戦中の東京大空襲で、多くの死傷者が出ました。

□20世紀、東京は関東大震災と東京大空襲で、二度の甚大な被害を受けました。

皇居内の正門石橋を臨む

江戸情緒

□下町を歩くと、昔ながらの江戸の生活を垣間見ることができます。

□東京の旧市街は、下町と呼ばれています。

□東京の旧市街は下町と呼ばれ、江戸の雰囲気が隅田川沿いに点々と残っています。

□東京の起源は江戸にあるので、東京を味わうには、江戸をよく知ることが大切です。

□江戸情緒は、今では浅草、谷中、両国、そして深川などの地域で見られます。

□東京の古い魅力を知るには、上野や浅草のような下町がおすすめです。

□浅草とその周辺は、今でも昔の江戸情緒を感じられる場所として知られています。

□浅草は東京でも最も人気のある観光スポットです。

□浅草の中心は、浅草寺です。

Tokyo suffered heavy casualties in the Tokyo air raids of World War II.

In the 20th century, Tokyo suffered severe damage twice, once from the Great Kanto Earthquake and once from the Tokyo air raids.

桜田門。江戸城（現在の皇居）の内堀に造られた門の一つ

Edo Nostalgia

Walking around downtown Tokyo, you can catch a glimpse of life in the old Edo period.

The old part of Tokyo is called *shitamachi*.

The old part of Tokyo is called *shitamachi*, and the atmosphere of Edo remains in areas dotting the Sumida River.

Since the origins of Tokyo lie in the city of Edo, a familiarity with Edo is crucial to appreciating Tokyo.

Now the atmosphere of Edo can be found in the Asakusa, Yanaka, Ryogoku, and Fukagawa areas of Tokyo.

The *shitamachi* areas in Tokyo found in the Ueno and Asakusa areas are recommended for their old-fashioned appeal.

Asakusa and its neighboring areas are famous as places where you can still feel the atmosphere of old Edo.

Asakusa is one of the most popular tourist spots in Tokyo.

Sensoji Temple is the heart of Asakusa.

□ 谷中とその周辺は、ぶらぶら歩くのにうってつけの場所です。

□ 谷中近辺の裏通りには、寺、工芸品店、レストラン、古い民家などが並び、江戸の味わいを楽しむことができます。

谷中の夕焼けだんだん

外国人にも人気の仲見世通り

□ 毎年、浅草寺には3000万の人が訪れます。

□ 浅草寺には観音菩薩が祀られています。

□ 浅草寺の参道は仲見世通りと呼ばれ、昔ながらの小物を買うことができます。

□ 浅草寺周辺では、伝統を生かした職人の手による工芸品に、浅草の真の良さを発見できます。

東京の観光スポット

□ 東京で最も大きい卸売市場である豊洲では、生き生きした仲買人たちのやり取りを見られるので、見逃さないように。

□ 豊洲は東京最大の卸売り市場として知られています。海産物の取扱量は世界最大です。

□ 東京の中で、新宿、池袋、渋谷は日本でも有数の繁華街です。

□ 原宿は渋谷に近く、若者文化発祥の地とされています。

□ 東京の六本木、青山周辺は、ナイトライフを楽しめる場所です。

□ 六本木、青山周辺には、国際色豊かなレストランや、しゃれた店がたくさんあります。

□ 東京では世界中の美味しい食事を楽しむことができます。

□ 東京では、伝統的な日本食だけでなく、世界中の料理を楽しむことができます。

□ 新宿の近くの新大久保周辺には、大きな韓国人街があります。

Yanaka and the surrounding area are perfect places to wander around.

The back streets around Yanaka are lined with temples, craft stores, restaurants, and old private homes, offering a taste of Edo.

Each year, Sensoji Temple attracts 30 million visitors.

Sensoji Temple enshrines the bodhisattva Kannon (Goddess of Mercy).

The approach to Sensoji Temple is called Nakamise-dori, where visitors can buy traditional small articles.

Around the area of Sensoji Temple, you can find the real attraction of Asakusa, the craftsmanship of artisans carrying on ancient traditions.

Sightseeing Spots in Tokyo

Don't miss Toyosu, the largest wholesale market in Tokyo, where you can watch lively middlemen interacting with each other.

Toyosu is known as the largest wholesale market in Tokyo. It handles the largest volume of seafood in the world.

Within Tokyo, Shinjuku, Ikebukuro, and Shibuya are some of the busiest areas in Japan.

Harakuju is an area near Shibuya and is famous as a launch site for youth culture.

The Roppongi and Aoyama areas of Tokyo are places to enjoy nightlife.

The Roppongi and Aoyama neighborhoods are home to many international restaurants and trendy stores.

In Tokyo, you can enjoy delicious food from all over the world.

In Tokyo, you can enjoy not only traditional Japanese cuisine, but also food from all over the world.

There is a large Korean neighborhood in the Shin-Okubo area near Shinjuku.

□新宿の近くの新大久保周辺は、大きな韓国人街があり、本格的な韓国料理が食べられます。

□渋谷と新宿は、活気のある商業地区で、ショッピングやナイトライフを楽しめます。

□銀座は東京を代表する高級商業地で、ブランド店や老舗の名店が立ち並んでいます。

□東京駅近くの大手町は、東京の金融街です。

東京のウォーターフロントは
新しい観光スポット

The Shin-Okubo area near Shinjuku is home to a large Korean district where you can enjoy authentic Korean cuisine.

Shibuya and Shinjuku are vibrant commercial districts with great shopping and nightlife.

Ginza is Tokyo's leading upscale commercial district, with brand-name stores and long-established names.

Otemachi, near Tokyo Station, is Tokyo's financial district.

京都

その昔、唐の都「長安」を模したといわれる京都は、世界中の人があこがれる観光スポットです。由緒ある寺社、四季折々の自然の楽しみ方など、見どころがいっぱいです。

京都の概要

□京都は、日本の主要な観光都市です。

□京都は昔、日本の首都でした。

□京都は794年から1869年の間、日本の首都でした。

□京都は盆地に位置しています。

□京都は内陸に位置しています。

□京都は東京の西、460キロのところに位置しています。

□東京から京都までは、新幹線で2時間15分かかります。

□大阪から京都までは、電車で30分ほどです。

□京都の人は、自分たちの歴史や伝統にとても誇りを持っています。

□京都は日本の中でも最も歴史的なところです。

□京都は古都であるだけでなく、日本の文化の中心です。

□歴史の街として知られている京都ですが、経済的にも重要なところです。

京都の象徴、京都タワー

Track 16

Kyoto Overview

Kyoto is one of Japan's main tourist cities.

Kyoto used to be the capital of Japan.

Kyoto was the capital of Japan from 794 to 1869.

Kyoto is located in a basin.

Kyoto is located inland.

Kyoto is located about 460 kilometers west of Tokyo.

It takes 2 hours and 15 minutes from Tokyo to Kyoto by Shinkansen.

It takes only 30 minutes from Osaka to Kyoto by commuter train.

The people of Kyoto are quite proud of their history and traditions.

Kyoto is the most historical city in Japan.

Kyoto is not only the ancient capital, but also the cultural center of Japan.

Even though it is known as a historical city, Kyoto is still important economically.

京都の観光

□ 忙しい現代社会に暮らす日本人にとって、京都は精神的な癒しの場でもあります。

□ 数えきれないほどの名所旧跡が京都にはあります。

□ 美しい庭のある古い寺、神社、別荘、伝統の家など、数えきれない名所旧跡が京都にはあります。

□ 京都は街の中も郊外も、ぶらぶら歩いて見て回るのに、絶好の場所です。

□ 京都には、街なかだけでなく、郊外にもたくさんの素晴らしい所があります。

□ 2019年には、8700万人以上の人が京都を訪れています。

□ 京都の名所旧跡や文化遺産には、毎年100万人以上の海外の人が訪れています。

□ 京都には3000以上の寺や神社があります。

□ 京都にある多くの建築物や庭は、国宝です。

□ 京都には、様々な仏教宗派の本部になっている寺が、数多くあります。

□ 長い間、首都だった京都は、無数の政治的事件や争いごとの現場となりました。

京都の歴史

□ 天皇が宮廷を京都に移したのは、794年のことでした。

□ 794年から1185年まで、京都で天皇家が統治していた時代を、平安時代といいます。

□ 鎌倉幕府が崩壊した1333年、後醍醐天皇は京都に新政府を樹立しました。

Tourism in Kyoto

For Japanese people living in today's busy modern society, Kyoto is a place of spiritual healing.

There are countless places of historic interest in Kyoto.

Old temples with beautiful gardens, shrines, villas, traditional houses, and countless other sites of historical interest can be found in Kyoto.

Kyoto is a great place to wander around and see both the city and its suburbs.

Kyoto has many wonderful places to visit, not only in the city, but also in the suburbs.

In 2019, more than 87 million people visited Kyoto.

More than one million international visitors come to Kyoto's historical and cultural heritage sites every year.

Kyoto is home to more than 3,000 temples and shrines.

Many of the buildings and gardens in Kyoto are national treasures.

There are many temples in Kyoto that serve as headquarters for various Buddhist sects.

For a long time, Kyoto, which was the capital, was the site of countless political incidents and conflicts.

History of Kyoto

The Emperor moved his court to Kyoto in 794.

The period from 794 to 1185, when the Emperors ruled in Kyoto, is called the Heian period.

In 1333, after the collapse of the Kamakura shogunate, Emperor Godaigo established a new government in Kyoto.

□ 京都の後醍醐天皇による新政府は、たった3年しか続きませんでした。

□ 1338年、足利尊氏が将軍に命じられ、京都に新しい幕府を開きました。

□ 京都は、1467年から1477年までの応仁の乱で、荒廃しました。

□ 1603年に徳川家康は将軍に任命され、江戸(現東京)に幕府を開きましたが、天皇は京都に残りました。

□ 徳川幕府崩壊の後、首都は京都から東京に移されました。

□ 今でも、京都御所と呼ばれる宮廷が京都にはあります。

□ 京都御所は、京都の中心地にあります。

□ 天皇家は、重要な儀式があるときはいつでも京都御所を訪れます。

□ 京都の二条城に行くと、見事な装飾の部屋を見ることができますが、そこは1867年に最後の将軍が政権を返上した場所でもあります。

京都の街歩き

□ 京都の下町では、古い家などが立ち並ぶ通りや路地を歩くことができます。

□ 古い商家を町屋といい、京都のあちこちにあります。

□ 京都の町屋では、いろいろな手工芸品や骨董品などを見ることができます。

□ 鴨川は京都の真ん中を流れています。

□ 京都の繁華街は河原町で、鴨川の西岸に位置しています。

The new government by Emperor Godaigo in Kyoto lasted only three years.

In 1338, Ashikaga Takauji was ordered by the Shogun to establish a new shogunate in Kyoto.

Kyoto was devastated by the Onin War between 1467 and 1477.

In 1603, when Tokugawa Ieyasu was appointed shogun, he founded his government in Edo, which is now called Tokyo, while the emperor's court remained in Kyoto.

After the fall of the Tokugawa shogunate, the capital was moved from Kyoto to Tokyo.

Even today, Kyoto is home to the Imperial Court, known as the Kyoto Gosho.

The Kyoto Gosho is located in the center of Kyoto.

The emperor's family visits Kyoto Gosho whenever an important celebration takes place.

If you visit Nijo-jo Castle in Kyoto, you can see the beautifully decorated offices where the last shogun made his decision to relinquish power in 1867.

Walking around Kyoto

In downtown Kyoto, you can walk through alleys and streets lined with old houses.

Old merchant houses are called *machiya*, and can be found throughout Kyoto.

In Kyoto's *machiya* houses, you can see various handicrafts and antiques.

The Kamo River runs through the center of Kyoto.

The downtown area of Kyoto is Kawaramachi, which is located on the west bank of the Kamo River.

□ 鴨川の西側には先斗町（ぽんとちょう）があり、古くからの料理屋が立ち並んでいます。

□ 祇園は京都の伝統的な歓楽街の中でも最も高級な界隈です。

□ 祇園は国の歴史保存地区で、古くからの民家、お茶屋、料理屋などがあります。

□ 京都では芸者のことを芸妓と呼びます。彼女たちは、伝統的なお茶屋や料理屋で働くプロの芸人です。

□ 舞妓はまだ修行中の芸妓のことで、祇園あたりでは着物を着て、髪を結った舞妓たちを見かけます。

□ 芸妓は遊女ではありません。芸妓とは洗練された身のこなしで、パトロンや大切な顧客を楽しませる女性のことです。

京都周辺

□ 東山は、京都東部の山がちな地域のことです。

□ 東山は、東部の山がちな地域で、古い寺院が並んでいます。

□ 清水寺から銀閣寺まで、東山地区には多くの有名な寺があります。

□ 北山地区は街の北西にあり、そこには有名な禅寺が点在しています。

□ 金閣寺、妙心寺、そして龍安寺は、北山地区にあります。

Ponto-cho is located on the west side of the Kamo River and is lined with traditional restaurants.

Gion is the most exclusive neighborhood in Kyoto's traditional entertainment district.

Gion is a national historic preservation district and is home to old private homes, teahouses, and restaurants.

In Kyoto, *geisha* are called *geiko*. They are professional entertainers working at traditional tea houses and restaurants.

A *maiko* is a *geiko* in training, and you will see them in their traditional kimonos and hairstyles in the Gion area.

A *geiko* is not a prostitute. A *geiko* is a woman who entertains her patrons and valued customers with a refined demeanor.

Around Kyoto

Higashiyama is a mountainous region in eastern Kyoto.

Higashiyama is the mountainous eastern area lined with old temples.

Many famous temples, including Kiyomizudera and Ginkakuji, are located in the Higashiyama area.

The Kitayama area is to the northwest of the city and is dotted with famous Zen temples.

Kinkakuji, Myoshinji, and Ryoanji are located in the Kitayama area.

□ 金閣寺は黄金の建築物として有名で、北山地区にあります。

□ 龍安寺は石庭で有名です。

□ 嵐山は、川の流域に点在する小さな寺を訪れたり、散策するにはうってつけの場所です。

□ いくつかの歴史的な家屋や寺を訪ねるには、予約が必要です。

Kinkakuji Temple is famous for its golden pavilion and is located in the Kitayama area.

Ryoanji Temple is famous for its stone garden.

Arashiyama is a great place to visit and explore the small temples that dot the river basin.

Reservations are required to visit some of the historic houses and temples.

龍安寺の石庭

大阪

日本の文化の中心地であった京都に近い大阪は、西日本最大の都市です。独自の食文化や芸能文化が発達したところでもあります。

大阪の概要

□ 大阪は東京から550キロ西のところに位置しています。

□ 東京と大阪の間は、新幹線で2時間半かかります。

□ 東京ー大阪間は、頻繁に電車が行き来しています。

□ 大阪は京都の近くです。

□ 大阪は、日本で2番目に大きな商業の中心地です。

□ 大阪とその周辺は、日本で2番目に大きな経済、ビジネスの中心地です。

大阪の交通

関西国際空港

□ 大阪の鉄道の玄関は新大阪駅で、大阪駅の北東5キロのところにあります。

□ 大阪の国際空港は街の約50キロ南にあり、関西国際空港といいます。

□ 大阪の国内線向け空港は、大阪国際空港（伊丹空港）といいます。

□ 淀川は京都から大阪、そして大阪湾へと流れ込み、そこには大阪港があります。

□ 神戸は港湾都市で大阪の西に位置しています。

Track 17

Overview of Osaka

Osaka is located about 550 kilometers west of Tokyo.

It takes two hours and thirty minutes to travel between Tokyo and Osaka by Shinkansen bullet train.

There are frequent trains between Tokyo and Osaka.

Osaka is located near Kyoto.

Osaka is the second-largest commercial center in Japan.

Osaka and its surrounding area make up the second-largest economic and business center in Japan.

Transportation in Osaka

Osaka's rail gateway is Shin-Osaka Station, located five kilometers northeast of Osaka Station.

Osaka's international airport is located about 50 kilometers south of the city and is named Kansai International Airport.

The airport for domestic flights in Osaka is called Osaka International Airport (Itami Airport).

The Yodo River flows from Kyoto to Osaka and into Osaka Bay, where the port of Osaka is located.

Kobe is a port city and is located west of Osaka.

□ 西から東へ、神戸、大阪、京都の3都市は、大阪都市圏を形成しています。

□ 大阪を中心とした広域圏を関西といいます。

□ 関西はかつて上方と言われていました。当時は天皇が住んでいるところを“上の方”としたからです。

大阪の人

□ 大阪市の人口は277万人です。

□ 大阪市の人口は277万人ですが、京都市、神戸市を含め周辺地域には約1900万の人が住んでいます。

□ 大阪弁とは、大阪の人が使う方言です。

□ 大阪の人たちは、大阪弁と言われるユニークな方言を使います。

□ 大阪の人たちは、東京の人より強い地元意識を持っています。

□ 大阪では、人々は自分たちのユーモアのセンスに誇りを持っていて、独特のお笑いエンターテインメントがあります。

大阪の歴史

□ 大阪が日本で最も重要な都市になったのは、100年にわたる内戦の後、豊臣秀吉が日本を統一し、大阪城を築いたときです。

□ 100年の内戦を経て、日本を統一し大阪城を築いた豊臣秀吉は、大阪の人に人気のヒーローです。

□ もともとの大阪城は、豊臣秀頼が徳川家康に滅ぼされた1615年に焼失しました。

□ 徳川家康は1603年、江戸（現東京）に幕府を開き、12年後に大阪城の豊臣秀頼を倒しました。

□ 江戸時代、大阪は西日本の商業、文化の中心として栄えました。

From west to east, Kobe, Osaka, and Kyoto form the Osaka Metropolitan Area.

The Greater Osaka Area is called Kansai.

Kansai used to be known as Kamigata. This is because at that time, the area where the emperor lived was called "*Kami-no-hou*".

Osaka's People

The population of Osaka City is 2.77 million.

Osaka City has a population of 2.77 million, but approximately 19 million people live in the surrounding area, including the cities of Kyoto and Kobe.

Osaka-ben is a dialect used by the people of Osaka.

The people of Osaka speak a unique dialect called *Osaka-ben*.

People in Osaka have a stronger sense of local identity than people in Tokyo.

Osaka people take pride in their sense of humor and have their own unique brand of comedic entertainment.

History of Osaka

Osaka became the most important city in Japan when Toyotomi Hideyoshi unified Japan and built Osaka Castle after a hundred years of civil war.

Toyotomi Hideyoshi, who unified Japan and built Osaka Castle after a hundred years of civil war, is a popular hero among the people of Osaka.

The original Osaka Castle was burned down in 1615 when Toyotomi Hideyori was defeated by Tokugawa Ieyasu.

Tokugawa Ieyasu established the shogunate in Edo (now Tokyo) in 1603 and defeated Toyotomi Hideyori at Osaka Castle 12 years later.

During the Edo period, Osaka flourished as the commercial and cultural center of western Japan.

□ 江戸時代、文楽が大阪で始まりました。

大阪らしさ

□ 大阪は商人魂で有名です。大阪の商人を「大阪商人」と呼びます。

□ 阪神タイガースは大阪地区をベースにする人気のプロ野球チームで、東京をベースにする読売ジャイアンツとはライバル同士です。

□ 大阪駅のある梅田は、大阪のビジネスの中心です。

□ 難波は大阪の商業の中心で、梅田の南側に位置しています。

□ 大阪・京都で発展した歌舞伎は、上方歌舞伎と呼ばれます。

大阪駅前

Bunraku (puppet theater) began in Osaka during the Edo period.

Osaka Characteristics

Osaka is famous for its merchant spirit. Osaka's merchants are called *Osaka-shonin*.

The Hanshin Tigers are a popular professional baseball team based in the Osaka area, and they are rivals with the Yomiuri Giants, who are based in Tokyo.

Umeda, where Osaka Station is located, is the business center of Osaka.

Namba is the commercial center of Osaka and is located south of Umeda.

Kabuki developed in Osaka and Kyoto is called *Kamigata kabuki*.

北海道

北海道は日本列島の最北端の島です。面積が広く、農業や畜産業が盛んです。冬は質のいい雪が降り、スキーリゾートには多くの海外からの観光客が集まっています。

北海道の概要

□ 北海道は日本の行政区のひとつです。

□ 北海道は日本の4つの主な島のうちのひとつです。

□ 北海道は日本の4つの主な島のうちのひとつで、本州のすぐ北に位置しています。

□ 北海道は日本で最も北にある島です。

□ 北海道は最も北にある島で、冬の寒さはとても厳しいです。

□ 北海道は日本で2番目に大きい島で、オーストリアと同じぐらいの大きさです。

□ 北海道は、アイルランド島と同じぐらいの大きさで、520万ほどの人が住んでいます。

□ 北海道は日本で2番目に大きい島で、人口はたった520万人です。

□ 北海道の冬はとても寒く、スキーリゾートもたくさんあります。

□ 北海道の北東側の沿岸には大量の流氷が流れ着き、見事です。

□ 北海道は広いので、空いている土地がたくさんあります。

□ 北海道は、日本の他の地域のように混んでいません。実際、空いている土地がたくさんあります。

Track 18

札幌の時計台

Overview of Hokkaido

Hokkaido is one of the administrative regions of Japan.

Hokkaido is one of the four main islands of Japan.

Hokkaido is one of the four main islands of Japan and is located just north of Honshu.

Hokkaido is the northernmost island of Japan.

Hokkaido is the most northerly island, and winters there are very cold.

Hokkaido is the second-largest island in Japan, and is about the same size as Austria.

Hokkaido is about the same size as the island of Ireland and is home to about 5.2 million people.

Hokkaido is the second-largest island in Japan with a population of only 5.2 million.

Winters in Hokkaido are very cold, and there are many ski resorts.

The northeastern coast of Hokkaido is spectacular, with large amounts of drift ice.

Hokkaido is large, and there is a lot of available land.

Hokkaido is not crowded like other parts of Japan. In fact, there is a lot of vacant land.

北海道の交通

□ 東京から北海道へ行くには、函館まで新幹線で行くのが便利です。約4時間15分で函館に着き、そこから在来線に乗り継ぐことができます。

□ 新千歳空港は、北海道の空の入り口です。

北方領土

□ 千島列島（クリル諸島）は、北東沿岸に位置しています。

□ クリル諸島の4島について、日本とロシア双方が領土だと主張し合っています。

アイヌの人々

□ 北海道にはアイヌという民族が住んでいます。

□ アイヌは日本の少数民族で、かつては日本の北部に広く居住していました。

□ アイヌは北海道の先住民族で、日本の他の地域には見られない独特な文化を持っています。

北海道の歴史

□ 北海道の大部分は19世紀に拓かれました。

□ 北海道への定住が始まったのは19世紀頃で、日本の他の地域と比べると大変遅いです。

□ 19世紀の北海道は開拓地でした。そのため、歴史的背景や雰囲気が他の日本の地域とはまったく違います。

十勝平野の雄大な風景

Transportation in Hokkaido

A convenient way to get to Hokkaido from Tokyo is to take the Shinkansen to Hakodate. It takes approximately 4 hours 15 minutes to reach Hakodate, from where you can connect to local lines.

New Chitose Airport is the air gateway to Hokkaido.

Northern Territories

The Kuril Islands are located off the northeast coast of Japan.

Both Japan and Russia claim the four Kuril Islands as their territory.

The Ainu People

Hokkaido is home to the Ainu people.

The Ainu are a small ethnic minority group in Japan that once lived throughout the northern part of the country.

The Ainu are the indigenous people of Hokkaido and have a unique culture not found elsewhere in Japan.

History of Hokkaido

Most of Hokkaido was settled in the 19th century.

Settlement in Hokkaido began around the 19th century, much later than in other parts of Japan.

Hokkaido was a frontier region in the 19th century. Therefore, its historical background and atmosphere are quite different from other parts of Japan.

札幌・函館

□ 札幌は北海道の道庁所在地です。

□ 札幌は北海道の道庁所在地であり、商業の中心です。

□ 札幌では2月初旬に雪祭りが行われ、野外にディスプレイされた雪の像などを楽しめます。

□ 函館は昔からの港町で、北海道の海からの玄関口となっています。

□ 函館は日本で最初に開かれた貿易港の一つで、西洋文化を取り入れた異国情緒あふれる街並みが現在も見られます。

札幌雪祭り

Sapporo and Hakodate

Sapporo is the capital of Hokkaido.

Sapporo is the capital and commercial center of Hokkaido.

Sapporo holds a snow festival in early February, where visitors can enjoy snow statues and other outdoor displays.

Hakodate is a traditional port town and the gateway to Hokkaido from the sea.

Hakodate was one of the first ports in Japan to be opened to international trade, and its streets still retain a unique exotic atmosphere influenced by Western culture.

函館五稜郭

東北地方

東北地方は別称として、「奥羽地方」「みちのく」と呼ばれることもあります。農業が盛んで、米や酒の産地も多く、海産物などの新鮮な味も楽しめます。青森は本州の最北端に位置しています。

東北地方の概要

□ 東北地方とは、本州の東北地域のことです。

□ 東北は本州東北部のことで、北海道とは津軽海峡で隔てられています。

□ 東北には6つの県があります。

□ 青森は本州の最北端に位置しています。

□ 秋田と山形は、日本海に面しています。

□ 岩手、宮城、そして福島は太平洋に面しています。

東北の交通

□ 東北と北海道は、青函トンネルで結ばれています。

□ 東北と北海道をつなぐのは、津軽海峡の下を通る青函トンネルです。

□ 現在、新幹線が東京と東北地方の各県庁所在地を結んでいます。

□ 東北は景色を楽しみながら列車の旅をするにはもってこいです。

□ 東北は山、湖、そして複雑に海岸線が入り組んでいることで知られる三陸海岸などが有名です。

Track 19

Overview of the Tohoku Region

The Tohoku region is the northeastern part of Honshu.

Tohoku is the northeastern part of Honshu, separated from Hokkaido by the Tsugaru Strait.

There are six prefectures in Tohoku.

Aomori is located in the northernmost part of Honshu.

Akita and Yamagata face the Sea of Japan.

Iwate, Miyagi, and Fukushima face the Pacific Ocean.

Transportation in Tohoku

Tohoku and Hokkaido are connected by the Seikan Tunnel.

The Seikan Tunnel, which passes under the Tsugaru Strait, connects Tohoku and Hokkaido.

Currently, the Shinkansen bullet train connects Tokyo to the prefectural capitals of the Tohoku region.

Tohoku is a great place for scenic train travel.

Tohoku is famous for its mountains, lakes, and the Sanriku Coast, known for its intricate coastline.

東北らしさ

□ 東北の人は、東北弁という方言を使います。

□ 東北弁は、東北の人たちが使っている独特な方言のことです。

□ 東北は夏祭りでよく知られています。

□ 仙台は七夕祭りで有名です。七夕祭りは２つの星座の伝説に基づいています。

□ 青森県のねぶた祭りは、豪華な装飾が施された山車がよく知られています。

□ 夏に秋田県で行われる竿燈（かんとう）祭りでは、長い竹竿にたくさんの提灯を吊り下げた大きな飾りを持って人々が練り歩きます。

□ 東北は民芸品で有名です。

□ 東北のこけしは、昔からの木製の人形で、主に山形で作られています。

毎年８月の初旬に行われる竿灯祭り

□ 座敷童は、子どもの幽霊のことです。座敷童は古い家々を害から守ると東北では言われています。

□ なまはげは、秋田地方の来訪神のことです。大晦日になまはげは家々を訪れ、親の言うことを聞くようにと子どもたちを怖がらせます。

青森県

□ 東北の最北の県は青森です。

□ 津軽は青森県の西部のことで、リンゴで有名です。

□ 十和田湖は青森県にあり、湖周辺は美しい山々、川の流れ、温泉などがあります。

岩木山と、その手前に見えるりんご畑

Tohoku Characteristics

People in Tohoku use a dialect called *Tohoku-ben.*

Tohoku-ben is a unique dialect used by the people of Tohoku.

Tohoku is well known for its summer festivals.

Sendai is famous for its Tanabata Festival. The Tanabata Festival is based on a legend about two constellations.

The Nebuta Festival in Aomori Prefecture is well known for its ornately decorated floats.

The Kanto Festival, held in Akita Prefecture in the summer, features a parade of people carrying large ornaments with many lanterns suspended from long bamboo poles.

Tohoku is famous for its folk crafts.

Kokeshi dolls in Tohoku are traditional wooden dolls, mostly made in Yamagata.

Zashiki-warashi is a ghost of a child. It is said in Tohoku that *Zashiki-warashi* protect old houses from harm.

Namahage are visiting deities in the Akita region. On New Year's Eve, *Namahage* visit houses to scare children into listening to their parents.

Aomori Prefecture

The northernmost prefecture in Tohoku is Aomori.

Tsugaru is the western part of Aomori Prefecture, famous for its apples.

Lake Towada is located in Aomori, and the area surrounding the lake has beautiful mountains, rivers, and hot springs.

秋田県

□ 秋田県は、東北の北西にあり、冬季の豪雪で知られています。

□ 田沢湖は秋田県の行楽地です。

□ 秋田県に行ったら、角館を訪ねてください。封建時代からの武家屋敷がよく保存されています。

岩手県

□ 盛岡は岩手県の県庁所在地で、かつては南部氏の所領でした。城跡は今でも街の中心に残っています。

□ 岩手県の太平洋側は三陸といい、風光明媚なリアス式海岸でよく知られています。

□ 遠野は岩手県にある村ですが、民間伝承で有名な町です。

□ 平泉は歴史のある町で、12世紀に権勢を振るった藤原氏の本拠地だったところです。

□ 岩手県の太平洋岸は、東日本大震災の津波で壊滅的な被害を受けました。

宮城県

□ 宮城県には仙台市があります。仙台は東北地方の中心です。

□ 仙台市は東北地方の中心で、この地域では最大の都市です。

□ 仙台市は、封建時代に最も勢力のあった家の一つ、伊達家の城下町です。

□ 仙台の青葉城は、封建時代に最も勢力の大きかった家の一つ、伊達家の居城でした。

Akita Prefecture

Akita Prefecture is located in the northwestern part of Tohoku and is known for its heavy snowfall in winter.

Lake Tazawa is a popular recreation spot in Akita Prefecture.

If you visit Akita Prefecture, be sure to go to Kakunodate. The samurai residences from the feudal era are well preserved.

Iwate Prefecture

Morioka is the capital of Iwate Prefecture and was once the seat of the Nanbu clan. The ruins of a castle still remain in the center of the city.

The Pacific side of Iwate Prefecture is called Sanriku and is well known for its scenic ria coastline.

岩手山を眺める

Tono is a village in Iwate Prefecture, and it is famous for its folklore.

Hiraizumi is a town with a long history and was the home of the Fujiwara Clan, which rose to power in the 12th century.

The Pacific coast of Iwate Prefecture was devastated by the tsunami following the Great East Japan Earthquake.

Miyagi Prefecture

Miyagi Prefecture is home to the city of Sendai. Sendai is the center of the Tohoku region.

Sendai is the center of the Tohoku region and the largest city in the area.

Sendai City is the castle town of the Date family, one of the most powerful families in the feudal era.

Aoba Castle in Sendai was the residence of one of the most powerful families in feudal times, the Date family.

□ 松島は宮城県の北部にある美しい海辺です。

白石川に映る宮城の象徴、蔵王山と桜

山形県

□ 山形県は秋田県の南に位置し、日本海に面しています。

□ 蔵王は山形県にある山で、スキーリゾートとして知られています。

□ 出羽三山は山形県にある3つの山で、古代より霊山として知られています。

福島県

□ 福島県は東北南部に位置し、県庁所在地は福島市です。

□ 会津若松はお城で有名です。

□ 西部にある会津地方では、美しい湖や山が楽しめます。

□ 会津地方は、1868年に徳川幕府終焉の際、激しい戦いが行われた場所です。

□ 福島県は、東日本大震災の津波で起きた福島第一原子力発電所のメルトダウンで、今でも苦しんでいます。

滝桜と呼ばれる福島三春町の桜

Matsushima is a beautiful seaside area in the northern part of Miyagi Prefecture.

Yamagata Prefecture

Yamagata Prefecture is located south of Akita Prefecture and faces the Sea of Japan.

Zao is a mountain in Yamagata Prefecture and is known as a ski resort.

Dewa Sanzan are three mountains in Yamagata Prefecture, which have been thought to be sacred since ancient times.

月山の山頂には月山神社が見える

Fukushima Prefecture

Fukushima Prefecture is located in the southern Tohoku region, and its capital is Fukushima City.

Aizu Wakamatsu is famous for its castle.

The Aizu region in the west offers beautiful lakes and mountains.

The Aizu region was the site of a fierce battle at the end of the Tokugawa Shogunate in 1868.

Fukushima Prefecture is still suffering from the meltdown of the Fukushima Daiichi Nuclear Power Plant caused by the tsunami that followed the Great East Japan Earthquake.

関東地方

関東には、日本の総人口の３分の１が集中しており、首都東京は日本の政治、経済、文化の中心です。東京では、2021年に２回目の夏のオリンピックが開催されました。

関東地方の概要

□ 関東は本州の東部中央に位置し、日本の中心です。

□ 関東地方に、東京があります。

□ 関東地方は東京都のほかに6県あります。

□ 横浜は東京の南に位置し、首都圏への海の玄関口となっています。

□ 横浜は東京の南に位置する大都市で、江戸時代終わりごろには外国人の居住区がありました。

□ 横浜には日本最大の中華街があります。

□ 関東北部の群馬県と栃木県の山沿いは、趣のある温泉街がたくさんあります。

□ 関東の南部から中部にかけて、関東平野が広がっています。

□ 関東北部から西部にかけては、山や温泉で有名です。

□ 伊豆諸島は、太平洋側にある伊豆半島から南に連なっています。

□ 千葉県の成田空港は東京の中心部から列車で1時間ほどのところにあります。

Track 20

Overview of the Kanto Region

Kanto is located in the center of the eastern part of Honshu, the main island of Japan, and is the most important part of Japan.

Tokyo is located in the Kanto region.

In addition to Tokyo, there are six prefectures in the Kanto region.

Yokohama is located south of Tokyo and is the ocean gateway to the Tokyo metropolitan area.

Yokohama is a large city located south of Tokyo and had a foreign settlement at the end of the Edo period.

Yokohama is home to Japan's largest Chinatown.

Along the mountains of Gunma and Tochigi Prefectures in the northern part of Kanto are many quaint hot spring resorts.

The Kanto Plain extends from southern to central Kanto.

The northern and western parts of Kanto are famous for mountains and hot springs.

The Izu Islands extend south from the Izu Peninsula on the Pacific Ocean side.

Chiba Prefecture's Narita Airport is about an hour's train ride from central Tokyo.

□ 東京の近くには2つの国際空港があります。一つが成田空港で、もう一つが東京の中心からすぐの海沿いにある羽田空港となります。

□ 羽田空港は、日本で最も面積の大きい国内線・国際線の空港です。

□ 成田で時間があれば、ぜひ成田市の新勝寺を訪ねてみてください。

成田空港にも近い、成田山新勝寺

東京近郊の観光

□ 東京周辺には、日光国立公園など、魅力的なところがたくさんあります。

□ 東京からたった2時間ほどのところにある日光は、日光東照宮という豪華な装飾の施された神社があり、人気があります。

□ 日光東照宮は、徳川家康が死んだ翌年の1617年に建立されました。

□ 東京にほど近い鎌倉は、1192年から1333年までの間、将軍が住んでいたところです。

□ 鎌倉にはたくさんの古寺や神社があり、訪ねてみるのもいいものです。

□ 1192年から1333年の間、将軍がいた鎌倉には古寺や神社がたくさんあり、興味深い場所です。

東京

□ 東京は東京都と呼ばれる特別行政区で、23区だけでなく、奥多摩など西部の山あいの地域も含まれています。

□ 太平洋に浮かぶ伊豆と小笠原諸島は、東京都に属し、都内から1000kmにわたって点在しています。

お台場側からのレインボーブリッジ風景

There are two international airports near Tokyo. One is Narita Airport, and the other is Haneda Airport, which is located along the coast, close to the center of Tokyo.

Haneda Airport is the largest domestic and international airport in Japan in terms of area.

If you have time in Narita, be sure to visit Shinshoji Temple in Narita City.

Sightseeing near Tokyo

There are many attractive places to visit around Tokyo, including Nikko National Park.

Nikko, located only two hours from Tokyo, is popular for its gorgeously decorated shrine, Nikko Toshogu.

Nikko Toshogu was built in 1617, the year after Tokugawa Ieyasu died.

Kamakura, near Tokyo, was home to the Shogun from 1192 to 1333.

There are many old temples and shrines in Kamakura that are worth visiting.

Kamakura, where the Shogun lived from 1192 to 1333, has many old temples and shrines that are interesting places to visit.

Tokyo

Tokyo is a special administrative district called Tokyo Metropolis, which includes not only the 23 wards but also mountainous areas in the west, such as Okutama.

The Izu and Ogasawara Islands in the Pacific Ocean are part of Tokyo and are scattered over 1,000 km from Tokyo.

群馬県

□ 群馬県は関東の北西に位置し、前橋市が県庁所在地です。

□ 群馬には、草津、伊香保、水上など多くの有名な温泉があります。

□ 草津や伊香保には、こじんまりした旅館が多く、日本らしい宿屋などが並ぶ温泉リゾート地です。

□ 群馬は昔、上州と呼ばれ、この地方の特長として乾燥した冬の風と、女性が活発でよく働くことで知られています。

栃木県

□ 栃木県は関東の中北部に位置し、県庁所在地は宇都宮市です。

□ 栃木県の山沿い地方に日光・那須など、日本でも最も人気のある観光地があります。

□ 面白いことに、栃木では餃子がよく食べられています。

徳川家康を祀る日光東照宮

茨城県

□ 茨城県は太平洋に面しており、県庁所在地の水戸には、偕楽園という伝統的な公園があります。

□ 筑波研究学園都市には数多くの研究施設が集まっています。

□ 茨城県の霞ヶ浦地方には多くの湖があります。

Gunma Prefecture

Gunma Prefecture is located in the northwestern part of the Kanto region, and Maebashi is the prefectural capital.

Gunma is home to many famous hot springs, including Kusatsu, Ikaho, and Minakami.

Kusatsu and Ikaho are hot spring resort areas with many small inns that are uniquely Japanese.

草津の湯もみは観光客にも人気

Gunma was once called Joshu, and the region is known for its dry winter winds and active, hard-working women.

Tochigi Prefecture

Tochigi Prefecture is located in the north-central part of the Kanto region, and its capital is Utsunomiya City.

Some of Japan's most popular tourist destinations, such as Nikko and Nasu, are located in the mountainous regions of Tochigi Prefecture.

Interestingly, *gyoza* (potstickers) are often eaten in Tochigi.

Ibaraki Prefecture

Ibaraki Prefecture faces the Pacific Ocean and has a traditional park called Kairakuen in Mito, the prefectural capital.

Tsukuba Science City is home to numerous research facilities.

There are many lakes in the Kasumigaura region of Ibaraki Prefecture.

偕楽園にある好文亭

埼玉県

□ 埼玉県は東京の北に位置し、首都圏に属しています。

□ 秩父と長瀞は、東京に住む人々にとってちょうどいい山あいのハイキングコースです。

□ 埼玉の県庁所在地はさいたま市です。

千葉県

□ 千葉県は東京の東に位置し、東京のベッドタウンになっています。

□ 千葉県の房総半島には、東京から多くの人がマリンスポーツを楽しみにやってきます。

□ 成田国際空港は千葉県にあり、東京から電車で約1時間ほどです。

神奈川県

□ 神奈川県は東京に隣接し、東京湾に面しています。

□ 横浜市は神奈川県の県庁所在地で、東京から電車で30分ほどです。

□ 神奈川県の横浜、鎌倉は、史跡なども多いところです。

□ 神奈川県は都内の人がマリンスポーツを楽しむ場所として人気です。

□ 箱根は、東京の近くにあって自然を満喫できる山間のリゾートです。

相模湾に面する湘南海岸

Saitama Prefecture

国指定の名勝、長瀞渓谷

Saitama Prefecture is located north of Tokyo and is part of the Tokyo Metropolitan Area.

Chichibu and Nagatoro are good mountain hiking trails for Tokyo residents.

Saitama's capital is Saitama City.

Chiba Prefecture

Chiba Prefecture is located east of Tokyo and is a bedroom community for Tokyo.

Many people from Tokyo come to the Boso Peninsula in Chiba Prefecture to enjoy marine sports.

Narita International Airport is located in Chiba Prefecture, about an hour from Tokyo by train.

Kanagawa Prefecture

Kanagawa Prefecture is adjacent to Tokyo and faces Tokyo Bay.

Yokohama City is the capital of Kanagawa Prefecture and is about 30 minutes from Tokyo by train.

Yokohama and Kamakura in Kanagawa Prefecture are places with many historical sites.

Kanagawa Prefecture is a popular place for people in Tokyo to enjoy marine sports.

Hakone is a mountain resort near Tokyo where visitors can enjoy nature.

中部地方

中部地方は広い地域を指すため、太平洋側の県と日本海側の県、または内陸に位置する県で、気候、方言、食事、習慣など地域による違いが大きいです。

中部地方の概要

□ 中部地方は本州中部の広い地域のことです。

□ 中部地方は日本海にも太平洋にも面しています。

□ 中部地方には9つの県があります。

□ 中部地方には9つの県があり、最大の都市は名古屋です。

□ 名古屋およびその周辺は、日本で3番目に大きな経済産業圏です。

□ 中部国際空港は、海外から名古屋への空の玄関口です。

□ 北陸地方の中心は金沢です。

富士山

□ 富士山は静岡県と山梨県の境にあり、その美しい姿で知られています。

□ 富士山は美しく雄大な火山として日本の象徴になっています。

□ 富士山は活火山で、標高3776mと日本一の高さです。

□ 空気が澄んでいるときは、東京からも富士山が見えます。

Track 21

Overview of the Chubu Region

The Chubu region is a large area in central Honshu.

The Chubu region faces both the Sea of Japan and the Pacific Ocean.

There are nine prefectures in the Chubu region.

There are nine prefectures in the Chubu region, and the largest city is Nagoya.

Nagoya and its surrounding area make up the third-largest economic and industrial area in Japan.

Chubu International Airport is the air gateway to Nagoya from abroad.

Kanazawa is the center of the Hokuriku region.

Mt. Fuji

Mt. Fuji is located on the border of Shizuoka and Yamanashi prefectures and is known for its beautiful appearance.

Fuji has become a symbol of Japan as a beautiful and majestic volcano.

Mt. Fuji is an active volcano and is the highest in Japan at 3,776 meters above sea level.

When the air is clear, Mt. Fuji can be seen from Tokyo.

日本アルプス

□ 中部地方には、日本アルプスという高い山脈がそびえています。

□ 日本アルプスでは、山での様々なレジャーを楽しめます。

□ 日本アルプス方面に行くには、山沿いを通り東京と名古屋を結ぶ中央線を使うのが便利です。

北陸

□ 北陸地方には北陸本線という列車が通っています。

□ 小松空港は、福井県と石川県の2県で使用されています。

□ 中部地方のうち北部を北陸地方といいます。

□ 中部地方の北部に位置し、日本海に面した北陸地方は、豪雪地帯として知られています。

□ 北陸地方は積雪の多さで知られていましたが、最近は温暖化の影響でそうでもありません。

静岡県

□ 静岡県は太平洋に面して広がっています。

□ 伊豆半島は富士山に近く、国立公園の一部でもあります。

□ 伊豆半島は比較的東京にも近く、温泉リゾートも数多くあります。

□ 伊豆半島の入口に熱海があり、温泉リゾートとしてとても有名です。

The Japan Alps

In the Chubu region, there is a high mountain range called the Japan Alps.

The Japanese Alps offer a variety of leisure activities in the mountains.

To reach the Japan Alps, it is convenient to use the Chuo Line, which runs along the mountains and connects Tokyo and Nagoya.

Hokuriku

The Hokuriku region is served by the Hokuriku Main Line, a train line.

Komatsu Airport serves Fukui and Ishikawa Prefectures.

The northern part of the Chubu region is called the Hokuriku region.

Located in the northern part of the Chubu region and facing the Sea of Japan, the Hokuriku region is known for its heavy snowfall.

The Hokuriku region used to be known for its heavy snowfall, but it has lessened recently due to global warming.

Shizuoka Prefecture

Shizuoka Prefecture stretches along the Pacific Ocean.

The Izu Peninsula is close to Mt. Fuji and is part of a national park.

The Izu Peninsula is relatively close to Tokyo and has many hot spring resorts.

Atami is located at the entrance of the Izu Peninsula and is very famous as a hot spring resort.

山梨県

□山梨県は静岡県の北に位置しています。

□甲府盆地は、高い山に囲まれ、山梨県の真ん中に位置しています。

□甲府市は山梨県の県庁所在地で、その周辺はブドウ畑があることで知られています。

信玄公ゆかりの武田神社

□富士五湖は、富士山の麓にある山と湖の観光地です。

長野県

□長野県は、日本アルプスの最高峰の山々が位置するところです。

□長野はウィンタースポーツを楽しむのに最適で、1998年には冬季オリンピックも開催されました。

□長野は昔は信濃と呼ばれ、今でもこの呼び方が使われることがよくあります。

□長野県の県庁所在地は長野市で、642年に善光寺が建てられたことから発展しました。

□松本市は城下町で、長野の主要都市のうちのひとつです。

□木曽は長野の山間の谷に位置し、封建時代からの古い宿場町が点在しています。

□木曽は木曽杉と呼ばれる日本産の杉で有名です。

Yamanashi Prefecture

Yamanashi Prefecture is located north of Shizuoka Prefecture.

The Kofu Basin is surrounded by high mountains and is located in the middle of Yamanashi Prefecture.

Kofu City is the capital of Yamanashi Prefecture, and the surrounding area is known for its vineyards.

Fujigoko is a scenic resort area at the foot of Mount Fuji, featuring mountains and lakes.

Nagano Prefecture

Nagano Prefecture is where the highest mountains of the Japanese Alps are located.

Nagano is a great place to enjoy winter sports, and it hosted the 1998 Winter Olympics.

Nagano used to be called Shinano, and this term is still often used today.

Nagano's capital is Nagano City, which developed after Zenkoji Temple was built in 642.

Matsumoto is a castle town and is one of the major cities in Nagano.

Kiso is located in a mountain valley in Nagano and is dotted with old inn towns dating back to the feudal era.

Kiso is famous for its Japanese cedar called *Kisosugi*.

新潟県

日本百名山のひとつ、妙高山

□新潟県は、日本海に面し、ロシア東部からの入口になっています。

□新潟市は新潟県の県庁所在地で、東京から上越新幹線を使えば簡単に行けます。

□長岡と新潟県の山沿いで、世界最深積雪を記録しました。

□新潟は封建時代には越後と呼ばれていました。

□佐渡は日本海に浮かぶ島で、かつては金山があることで知られていました。

富山県

□富山市は富山県の県庁所在地で、日本海の富山湾に面しています。

□立山連峰は、登山のほかにスキーリゾートとしても知られています。

□富山周辺はイカやカニなどの海産物が豊富です。

市街から立山連峰を眺める

□富山の山間には昔ながらの集落が残っています。五箇山もそのひとつで、世界遺産に登録されています。

石川県

□金沢は北陸地方にある町で、史跡がたくさんあります。

□金沢は北陸地方にある町で、日本庭園で知られる兼六園や武家屋敷など、史跡がたくさんあります。

□金沢は、江戸時代に権勢を振るった前田家が統治していた歴史的な町です。

□金沢では洗練された見事な工芸品を見ることができます。その一つが日本の焼き物である九谷焼です。

Niigata Prefecture

Niigata Prefecture faces the Sea of Japan and is the gateway to eastern Russia.

Niigata City is the capital of Niigata Prefecture and can be easily reached from Tokyo by the Joetsu Shinkansen bullet train.

The world's deepest snowfall was recorded in Nagaoka and along the mountains of Niigata Prefecture.

Niigata was called Echigo in feudal times.

Sado is an island in the Sea of Japan and was once known for its gold mines.

Toyama Prefecture

Toyama City is the capital of Toyama Prefecture and faces Toyama Bay on the Sea of Japan.

The Tateyama mountain range is known as a ski resort and also for mountain climbing.

The area around Toyama is rich in seafood, such as squid and crabs.

Traditional villages still remain in the mountains of Toyama. Gokayama is one of them and is registered as a World Heritage site.

Ishikawa Prefecture

Kanazawa is a town in the Hokuriku region and has many historical sites.

Kanazawa is a city located in the Hokuriku region, famous for its Japanese gardens, such as Kenrokuen, and many historical sites like samurai residences.

Kanazawa is a historical town that was ruled by the Maeda family, which was a powerful clan during the Edo period (1603-1868).

In Kanazawa, one can see sophisticated and splendid crafts. One such example is Kutaniyaki, a kind of Japanese pottery.

雪つりがなされた名勝兼六園

□加賀友禅と呼ばれる染め物は、金沢の工芸品として有名です。

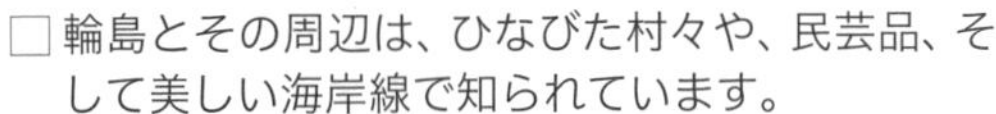

□輪島とその周辺は、ひなびた村々や、民芸品、そして美しい海岸線で知られています。

福井県

□福井県は京都の北に位置し、県庁所在地の福井市は城下町です。

□福井県の県庁所在地の福井市の近くには、禅宗の一派である曹洞宗の大本山である永平寺があります。

□福井は、東尋坊という岩だらけの細く伸びた海岸で有名です。

岐阜県

□長野と同様に、岐阜県も内陸の山地をまたぐようにして広がっています。

□岐阜県の白川郷は、茅葺きの急勾配の屋根の家があることで知られており、世界遺産にも登録されています。

□飛騨は、岐阜県の山間地方で、高山市はこの谷に古くからある町です。

白川郷の合掌造りの集落

Dyed fabrics known as Kaga Yuzen are a well-known Kanazawa craft.

Wajima and its surrounding area are known for the rustic villages, folk art, and beautiful coastline there.

Fukui Prefecture

Fukui Prefecture is located north of Kyoto, and Fukui City, the prefectural capital, is a castle town.

Near Fukui City, the prefectural capital, is Eiheiji Temple, the main temple of the Soto sect of Zen Buddhism.

九頭竜川河口にある景勝地、東尋坊

Fukui is famous for Tojinbo, a narrow stretch of rocky coastline.

Gifu Prefecture

Like Nagano, Gifu Prefecture straddles the inland mountains.

Shirakawa-go in Gifu Prefecture is known for its steeply pitched thatched roof houses and is a World Heritage site.

Hida is a mountainous region of Gifu Prefecture, and Takayama City is an old town in this valley.

愛知県

□ 中部地方の中心は名古屋です。名古屋とその周辺で、日本第3の経済圏を形成しています。

□ 名古屋とその周辺地域は、東京、大阪に次ぐ、日本で3番目の商業地区です。

□ 名古屋は愛知県にあり、かつて尾張と呼ばれていました。

□ 江戸時代の尾張は、将軍に最も近い親戚によって治められていました。

□ 名古屋までは、東京から新幹線で1時間半で行けます。

Aichi Prefecture

Nagoya is the center of the Chubu region. Nagoya and its surrounding area make up Japan's third-largest economic zone.

Nagoya and its surrounding area make up the third-largest commercial district in Japan, after Tokyo and Osaka.

Nagoya is located in Aichi Prefecture and was once called Owari.

During the Edo period, Owari was ruled by the closest relatives of the shogun.

Nagoya can be reached in 1.5 hours from Tokyo by Shinkansen bullet train.

金の鯱鉾から、金城とも称される名古屋城

近畿地方

関西地方ともいいます。長い間、日本の首都（都）がおかれていたこともあり、日本の伝統的な歴史や文化の中心地でもあります。日本の世界文化遺産の半分近くが、近畿地方にあるといわれるほどです。

近畿地方の概要

□ 近畿地方は、かつては日本の政治的、文化的中心でした。

□ 京都が位置しているのが近畿地方です。

□ 近畿地方最大の都市は大阪です。

□ 大阪とその周辺地域は、東京に次いで、日本で2番目に大きい商業地区です。

□ 京都は大阪の北東に位置しており、電車で簡単に行くことができます。

□ 近畿地方とは、名古屋の西、岡山県の東になります。

□ 近畿地方には5つの県と、2つの特別区があります。

□ 大阪、京都、神戸が近畿地方で最も大きな都市で、大阪経済圏を成しています。

□ 紀伊半島という大きな半島には、深い山や谷があり、その美しい海岸線を電車でも楽しむことができます。

□ 名古屋の西から、南方向へ伸びる紀伊半島から、日本の多くの古代史が始まりました。

□ 紀伊半島にはいくつかとても重要な神社や寺があります。こうした場所を結ぶ巡礼の道を熊野古道といいます。

□ 紀伊半島の東側には伊勢神宮という神社があります。

Track 22

Overview of the Kinki Region

The Kinki region was once the political and cultural center of Japan.

Kyoto is located in the Kinki region.

Osaka is the largest city in the Kinki region.

Osaka and its surrounding area make up the second-largest commercial district in Japan, after Tokyo.

Kyoto is located to the northeast of Osaka and is easily accessible by train.

The Kinki region is west of Nagoya and east of Okayama Prefecture.

The Kinki region includes five prefectures and two special wards.

Osaka, Kyoto, and Kobe are the largest cities in the Kinki region and form the Osaka economic zone.

The Kii Peninsula, a large peninsula, has deep mountains and valleys, and its beautiful coastline can be enjoyed by train.

Much of Japan's ancient history began on the Kii Peninsula, which stretches from the west of Nagoya in a southerly direction.

There are several very important shrines and temples on the Kii Peninsula. The pilgrimage route connecting these places is called Kumano Kodo.

On the eastern side of the Kii Peninsula is a shrine called Ise Jingu.

□ 伊勢神宮は皇室にとっての氏神で、日本でも最も崇拝されるところの一つです。

□ 伊勢神宮は約2000年前に建てられました。

□ 紀伊半島の中央部を大和と呼び、そこに古代の朝廷がありました。

□ 大和地方は日本の国が誕生したところとされています。

□ 大和地方には、1500年以上前の古墳、寺、神社などが多く残っています。

近畿地方の交通

□ 近畿地方を訪れるには、新幹線が便利です。

□ 直接近畿地方に入りたい人には、関西国際空港が玄関口です。

□ 近鉄（電車）は奈良、大和、伊勢間を効率よく結んでいます。

□ 近鉄（電車）は大阪、奈良、京都、三重、愛知を結ぶ便利な私鉄です。

大阪

□ 大阪は大阪府とよばれ、日本で2番目に大きい経済の中心地です。

1615年に焼失後、江戸期に再建された大阪城

京都

□ 京都は京都府とよばれ、京都市が県庁所在地です。

□ 京都府の北端には景観の美しい若狭湾があり、日本海に面しています。

The Ise Jingu is the clan deity for the imperial family and is one of the most revered places in Japan.

Ise Jingu was built about 2,000 years ago.

The central part of the Kii Peninsula is called Yamato, and is where the ancient Imperial Court was located.

The Yamato region is considered to be the birthplace of the Japanese nation.

In the Yamato region, there are many ancient burial mounds, temples, and shrines that are more than 1,500 years old.

Transportation in the Kinki Region

The Shinkansen bullet train is the most convenient way to visit the Kinki region.

Kansai International Airport is the gateway for those wishing to enter the Kinki region directly.

Kintetsu trains provide efficient connections between Nara, Yamato, and Ise.

Kintetsu is a convenient private railway connecting Osaka, Nara, Kyoto, Mie, and Aichi.

Osaka

Osaka is called Osaka-fu and is the second-largest economic center in Japan.

Kyoto

Kyoto is known as Kyoto-fu, and Kyoto City is the prefectural capital.

At the northern end of Kyoto Prefecture is the scenic Wakasa Bay, which faces the Sea of Japan.

日本三景のひとつ、天橋立

□ 京都府の北には、深い杉の森林が広がっています。

奈良県

□ 奈良県は紀伊半島の真ん中あたりに位置し、奈良市が県庁所在地です。

□ 奈良は日本でも指折りの歴史の町で、710年から784年までの間、都が置かれていたところです。

□ 奈良は京都から簡単に行けます。電車で京都駅から30分ほどです。

□ 奈良の古の都は、平城京といいます。

□ 奈良では8世紀に建立された東大寺に行くのがよいでしょう。

□ 東大寺は、752年に完成した世界最大の銅製の大仏で有名です。

□ 東大寺のほかにも、奈良にはたくさんの古い寺があります。

□ 奈良西部には、680年に建立された薬師寺があります。

□ 薬師寺は美しい三重塔が有名で、これは730年に建てられたものです。

□ 法隆寺は世界で最も古い木造建築で、607年に完成しました。

□ 奈良地方にある東大寺、薬師寺、法隆寺など多くの寺には、中国文化の影響が強く見られます。

明日香村の石舞台古墳

Deep cedar forests extend to the north of Kyoto Prefecture.

Nara Prefecture

Nara Prefecture is located in the middle of the Kii Peninsula, and Nara City is the prefectural capital.

Nara is one of the most historic cities in Japan and was the site of the capital from 710 to 784.

Nara is easily accessible from Kyoto. It takes about 30 minutes from Kyoto Station by train.

The ancient capital of Nara is called Heijokyo.

A good place to visit in Nara is Todaiji Temple, which was built in the 8th century.

Todaiji Temple is famous for having the world's largest bronze statue of the Great Buddha, completed in 752.

In addition to Todaiji, Nara has many other old temples.

In western Nara, there is Yakushiji Temple, which was built in 680.

Yakushiji Temple is famous for its beautiful three-story pagoda, which was built in 730.

Horyu-ji Temple is the oldest wooden structure in the world, completed in 607.

Many temples in the Nara region, including Todai-ji, Yakushi-ji, and Horyu-ji, are strongly influenced by Chinese culture.

和歌山県

□ 和歌山県は紀伊半島の西に位置し、和歌山市が県庁所在地です。

□ 和歌山の南部は太平洋に面しており、温暖な気候で知られています。

□ 和歌山は紀州と呼ばれて、かつては将軍の親戚の領地でした。

□ 和歌山県には高野山という山があり、そこは日本の密教である真言宗の総本山です。

高野山には真言宗の総本山、金剛峰寺がある

□ 高野山は、真言宗の総本山がある山の名前で、真言宗は9世紀初頭に有名な弘法大師によって開かれました。

三重県

□ 三重県は奈良県の東に位置し、名古屋にも近いです。県庁所在地は津市です。

□ 三重県の東海岸にある伊勢志摩地方は、神道でも最も神聖な場所として知られています。伊勢神宮もここにあります。

□ 伊勢志摩の海岸に沿って、たくさんの真珠養殖場があります。

兵庫県

□ 兵庫県は大阪の西に位置しています。

□ 神戸は兵庫県の県庁所在地で、日本で最も重要な港のひとつです。

□ 神戸は、1995年の阪神淡路大震災で大きな被害を受けました。

Wakayama Prefecture

Wakayama Prefecture is located in the west of the Kii Peninsula, and Wakayama City is the prefectural capital.

The southern part of Wakayama faces the Pacific Ocean and is known for its mild climate.

Wakayama is called Kishu, and was once the territory of a relative of the shogun.

Wakayama Prefecture is home to a mountain called Mt. Koya, which is the head temple of the Shingon sect of esoteric Buddhism in Japan.

Mt. Koya is the name of the mountain where the head temple of the Buddhist Shingon sect is located. It was founded by the famous Kobo Daishi in the early 9th century.

Mie Prefecture

Mie Prefecture is located east of Nara Prefecture and close to Nagoya. The prefectural capital is Tsu City.

The Ise-Shima region on the east coast of Mie Prefecture is known as the holiest place in Shintoism. The Ise Jingu Shrine is also located there.

There are many pearl farms along the coast of Ise-Shima.

二見町の夫婦岩

Hyogo Prefecture

Hyogo Prefecture is located west of Osaka.

Kobe is the capital of Hyogo Prefecture and one of the most important ports in Japan.

Kobe was severely damaged in the Great Hanshin-Awaji Earthquake of 1995.

□ 淡路島は瀬戸内海で最大の島で､本州とは明石海峡大橋でつながっています。

□ 淡路島は大鳴門橋で､四国の徳島ともつながっています。

□ 明石海峡大橋は, 世界最長の吊り橋です。

国の重要文化財にも指定される姫路城（白鷺城）

□ 姫路は姫路城という美しいお城があることで知られています。

滋賀県

□ 滋賀県の中央部には、日本最大の湖である琵琶湖があります。

□ 滋賀県は、文化的にも経済的にも京都や大阪との結びつきが強い地域です。

□ 彦根城の天守は国宝で、城の周囲は特別史跡に指定されています。

Awaji Island is the largest island in the Seto Inland Sea and is connected to Honshu by the Akashi Kaikyo Bridge.

Awaji Island is also connected to Tokushima in Shikoku via the Onaruto Bridge.

The Akashi Kaikyo Bridge is the world's longest suspension bridge.

Himeji is known for the beautiful Himeji Castle.

Shiga Prefecture

Lake Biwa, the largest lake in Japan, is located in the center of Shiga Prefecture.

Shiga Prefecture has strong cultural and economic ties with Kyoto and Osaka.

The Hikone Castle keep is a national treasure, and the area surrounding the castle is designated as a special historic site.

琵琶湖の眺め

中国地方

山陰（日本海側）と山陽（瀬戸内海側）では、気候、風習、食なども大きく違います。温暖な山陽と違い、山陰の一部は豪雪地帯でもあります。

中国地方の概要

□ 中国地方は本州の西の地域です。

□ 中国地方は近畿地方の西に位置しています。

□ 中国地方は瀬戸内海という海域に沿って広がっています。

□ 中国地方は関西と九州の間に位置しています。

□ 中国地方には5つの県があります。

□ 中国地方で一番大きいのは広島市です。

山陽・山陰

□ 中国地方の南、瀬戸内海に面した側を山陽と言います。

□ 中国地方の島根県と鳥取県は、日本海に面しています。

□ 山陽の主な都市には、新幹線で行くことができます。

□ 山陽新幹線は、山陽地方の都市を経由しながら、大阪と九州を結んでいます。

□ 東京から広島までは、新幹線で4時間半です。

Track 23

Overview of the Chugoku Region

The Chugoku region is located to the west of Honshu.

The Chugoku region is located west of the Kinki region.

The Chugoku region extends along the Seto Inland Sea.

The Chugoku region is located between Kansai and Kyushu.

There are five prefectures in the Chugoku region.

The largest city in the Chugoku Region is Hiroshima.

Sanyo and San'in

The southern part of the Chugoku region, facing the Seto Inland Sea, is called Sanyo.

Shimane and Tottori prefectures in the Chugoku region face the Sea of Japan.

Major cities in Sanyo can be reached by Shinkansen bullet train.

The Sanyo Shinkansen bullet train connects Osaka and Kyushu via cities in the Sanyo region.

It takes 4 hours and 30 minutes to get from Tokyo to Hiroshima by Shinkansen bullet train.

□ 中国地方の北部は日本海に面しており、山陰と呼ばれています。

瀬戸内海

□ 瀬戸内海は本州と四国の間にあります。

□ 瀬戸内海は本州と四国を隔てていますが、橋で行き来できます。

□ 瀬戸内海は重要な海の交通ルートであるだけでなく、小さな島が点在する景観の美しいところです。

□ 瀬戸内海には無数の静かな漁村が点在しています。

広島県

□ 広島県は、山口県と岡山県に挟まれ、県庁所在地は広島市です。

□ 広島県には、世界遺産が2つあります。一つは広島平和記念公園で、もう一つが厳島神社です。

□ 広島市は、1945年に原爆で破壊された街として世界中で知られています。

海上に立つ珍しい神社、厳島神社

□ 1945年8月6日、原爆が広島市上空で爆発し、およそ9万人がその日のうちに亡くなりました。

□ 20万人以上の人が広島の原爆で亡くなりました。

□ 広島では多くの人が放射能による健康被害に苦しみました。

□ 第二次世界大戦後、広島市は平和都市となりました。

□ 今では広島市は、この地方の商業・産業の中心地で、100万人以上の人が住んでいます。

The northern part of the Chugoku region faces the Sea of Japan and is called the San'in region.

Seto Inland Sea

The Seto Inland Sea lies between Honshu and Shikoku.

The Seto Inland Sea separates Honshu and Shikoku, but bridges can be used to go back and forth.

The Seto Inland Sea is not only an important sea transportation route but also an area of scenic beauty dotted with small islands.

The Seto Inland Sea is dotted with countless quiet fishing villages.

Hiroshima Prefecture

Hiroshima Prefecture is located between Yamaguchi and Okayama Prefectures, and its capital is Hiroshima City.

Hiroshima Prefecture has two World Heritage Sites. One is the Hiroshima Peace Memorial Park, and the other is Itsukushima Shrine.

Hiroshima City is known throughout the world as a city that was destroyed by the atomic bomb in 1945.

On August 6, 1945, an atomic bomb exploded over the city of Hiroshima, killing approximately 90,000 people on the day of bombing.

More than 200,000 people died as a result of the Hiroshima bombing.

Many people in Hiroshima suffered from health problems caused by radiation.

After World War II, Hiroshima City became a city that promotes peace.

Today, Hiroshima City is the commercial and industrial center of the region and is home to more than one million people.

鳥取県

□鳥取県は日本海に面し、県庁所在地は鳥取市です。

□鳥取市の海岸には、鳥取砂丘という大きな砂丘があります。

□米子近辺は、鳥取県の産業の中心です。

島根県

□島根県は日本海に面し、鳥取県の西に位置しています。

□松江市は島根県の県庁所在地で、城下町として知られています。

□19世紀後半、松江は作家でジャーナリストのラフカディオ・ハーン（小泉八雲）によってアメリカに紹介されました。

□出雲には出雲大社という重要な神社があり、ここは日本神話の時代まで遡ることができます。

岡山県

□岡山県は広島の東に位置し、県庁所在地は岡山市です。

□岡山県の南部は瀬戸内海に面しています。

回遊式庭園で知られる後楽園

Tottori Prefecture

日本海海岸に広がる鳥取砂丘

Tottori Prefecture faces the Sea of Japan, and its capital is Tottori City.

On the coast of Tottori City are large sand dunes called the Tottori Sand Dunes.

The area around Yonago is the center of industry in Tottori Prefecture.

Shimane Prefecture

Shimane Prefecture faces the Sea of Japan and is located west of Tottori Prefecture.

Matsue City is the capital of Shimane Prefecture and is known as a castle town.

In the late 19th century, Matsue was introduced to America by writer and journalist Lafcadio Hearn (Koizumi Yakumo).

Izumo is home to an important shrine, Izumo Taisha, which dates back to the time of Japanese mythology.

Okayama Prefecture

Okayama Prefecture is located east of Hiroshima, and its capital is Okayama City.

The southern part of Okayama Prefecture faces the Seto Inland Sea.

山口県

□ 山口県は本州の西の端に位置し、九州とは関門橋で結ばれています。

□ 山口県は封建時代には長州と呼ばれ、明治維新をもたらすのに重要な役割を果たした大藩でした。

□ 萩は長州の昔の都で、興味深い史跡がたくさんあります。

□ 山口県の下関は、中国地方の西の端に位置し、関門海峡を挟んで、九州と対峙しています。

本州と九州を分かつ関門海峡

Yamaguchi Prefecture

Yamaguchi Prefecture is located at the western end of Honshu and is connected to Kyushu by the Kanmon Bridge.

Yamaguchi Prefecture was known as Choshu in feudal times and was a large domain that played an important role in bringing about the Meiji Restoration.

Hagi was the old capital of Choshu and has many interesting historical sites.

Shimonoseki in Yamaguchi Prefecture is located on the western edge of the Chugoku region, facing Kyushu across the Kanmon Straits.

四国地方

四国は、日本の主要４島の中では一番小さな島です。四方を海に囲まれ、温暖な気候で、果物の生産が盛んです。

四国地方の概要

□ 日本の4つの主要な島の中で、四国が一番小さいです。

□ 四国は、中国地方の南、瀬戸内海を渡ったところに位置しています。

□ 四国は大阪の南西に位置しています。

□ 四国には4つの県があり、すべての県が海に面しています。

□ 四国は本州四国連絡橋という橋で行き来することができます。

□ 四国はその温暖な気候と山地で知られています。

□ 四国はミカンと海産物が有名です。

四国の交通

□ 中国地方の岡山から、瀬戸内海を渡る列車で、四国に行くことができます。

□ 四国に行くには、多くの人が新幹線で岡山まで行き、四国行きの電車に乗り換えます。

□ 四国のすべての県庁所在地の近くには空港があり、東京や大阪から飛行機で行けます。

Track 24

Shikoku Region Overview

Of the four main islands of Japan, Shikoku is the smallest.

Shikoku is located south of the Chugoku region, across the Seto Inland Sea.

Shikoku is located southwest of Osaka.

Shikoku has four prefectures, all of which face the sea.

Shikoku is accessible via the Honshu-Shikoku Bridge Project.

Shikoku is known for its mild climate and mountainous terrain.

Shikoku is famous for its tangerines and seafood.

Transportation in Shikoku

Shikoku can be reached from Okayama in the Chugoku region by train across the Seto Inland Sea.

To get to Shikoku, most people take the Shinkansen to Okayama and transfer to a train bound for Shikoku.

There are airports near all prefectural capitals in Shikoku, and you can fly from Tokyo or Osaka.

四国らしさ

☐ 四国生まれの僧である空海は、日本でも最も影響のある密教の一つ、真言宗を開きました。

☐ 空海は弘法大師とも呼ばれ、今の香川県、讃岐で774年に生まれました。

☐ 四国は、空海ゆかりの88ヵ所のお寺を回る四国お遍路という巡礼で有名です。

☐ 多くの日本人が、四国88ヵ所を歩いて周る巡礼の旅に出かけます。

☐ 四国88ヵ所を周る巡礼者のことを、日本語でお遍路さんと呼びます。

☐ お遍路は、日本人に人気の巡礼の旅で、全長1200キロ以上あります。

愛媛県

本州と四国を結ぶ来島大橋

☐ 愛媛県は、四国の北西に位置し、県庁所在地は松山市です。

☐ 松山は四国で最大の都市です。

☐ 道後は、松山市にほど近い温泉地として有名です。

☐ 石鎚山は、西日本で最も高い山で、仏教の修行の場として有名です。

香川県

☐ 香川県は四国の北東に位置し、県庁所在地は高松市です。

☐ 岡山から本州四国連絡橋を通って高松まで列車で行けるようになり、とても便利になりました。

☐ 香川県は、讃岐うどんと呼ばれる麺で有名です。

金比羅宮の参道

Shikoku Characteristics

Kukai, a Shikoku-born monk, founded the Shingon sect, one of the most influential esoteric religions in Japan.

Kukai, also known as Kobo Daishi, was born in 774 in Sanuki, in what is now Kagawa Prefecture.

Shikoku is famous for the Shikoku Pilgrimage, a pilgrimage to 88 temples associated with Kukai.

Many Japanese people go on pilgrimages to the 88 temples of Shikoku on foot.

Pilgrims who visit the 88 temples of Shikoku are called "*Ohenro-san*" in Japanese.

The *Ohenro* is a popular pilgrimage among Japanese people and is over 1,200 kilometers long.

Ehime Prefecture

Ehime Prefecture is located in the northwest of Shikoku, and its capital is Matsuyama City.

Matsuyama is the largest city in Shikoku.

Dogo is a famous hot spring resort near Matsuyama City.

Ishizuchi, the highest mountain in western Japan, is famous as a place for Buddhist ascetic practices.

Kagawa Prefecture

Kagawa Prefecture is located in the northeast of Shikoku, and its capital is Takamatsu City.

It is now very convenient to take a train from Okayama to Takamatsu via the Honshu-Shikoku Bridge Project.

Kagawa Prefecture is famous for its noodles called *Sanuki udon*.

□ 香川県は晴天の日が多く、雨量が少ないです。

徳島県

大小の渦巻ができる鳴門海峡

□ 徳島県は四国東部に位置し、県庁所在地は徳島市です。

□ 徳島市までは、瀬戸内海を渡る大きな吊り橋を使うと、大阪や神戸から車で簡単に行けます。

□ 鳴門海峡は、流れの速い渦潮で有名です。

高知県

□ 高知県は四国の南側で、県庁所在地は高知市です。

□ 高知県は太平洋に面し、黒潮と呼ばれる海流のおかげで温暖です。

□ 高知県は四国の南部にあり、温暖な気候で知られています。

□ 高知はかつて土佐と呼ばれ、封建時代には山内氏が統治していました。

□ 高知では、カツオやマグロなどの海の幸を楽しめます。

□ 気候が温暖なので、高知では年に2度、米が収穫できます。

Kagawa Prefecture has many sunny days and little rainfall.

Tokushima Prefecture

Tokushima Prefecture is located in the eastern part of Shikoku, and its capital is Tokushima City.

Tokushima City can be easily reached by car from Osaka or Kobe by using a large suspension bridge across the Seto Inland Sea.

The Naruto Strait is famous for its fast-flowing whirlpools.

Kochi Prefecture

Kochi Prefecture is located in the south of Shikoku, and its capital is Kochi City.

Kochi faces the Pacific Ocean and is warm thanks to the Kuroshio Current.

Kochi Prefecture is located in the southern part of Shikoku and is known for its mild climate.

Kochi was once called Tosa and was ruled by the Yamauchi clan during the feudal era.

In Kochi, visitors can enjoy seafood, such as bonito and tuna.

Because of the mild climate, rice is harvested twice a year in Kochi.

高知市街を臨む

九州地方

九州はアジアに近いので、古代には中国や韓国の無数の技術や文化の受け入れ口でした。日本の最西端に位置する沖縄は、363の島からなる県で、亜熱帯の気候をいかしたマリンスポーツなどの観光が盛んです。

九州地方の概要

□九州は日本の4つの島のうち、最も南に位置しています。

□九州は冬は暖かく、夏は暑いです。

□九州地方の商業の中心は福岡市です。

□九州と本州の間には関門海峡があります。

□九州には多くの火山、温泉があり、美しい景観の海岸線も楽しめます。

□九州には沖縄も含め8つの県があります。

□福岡市と北九州市は、九州の中でも最大のメガシティで、両市とも福岡県にあります。

九州の交通

□九州には東京から新幹線で行けます。所要時間は約5時間です。

□2011年、新幹線は、九州の最南端の県、鹿児島まで延長されました。

□東京から九州までは飛行機で1時間半かかります。

□九州は大陸に近いので、何世紀もの間、日本への玄関口でした。

Track 25

Kyushu Region

Kyushu is the southernmost of Japan's four islands.

Kyushu has warm winters and hot summers.

The commercial center of the Kyushu region is Fukuoka City.

The Kanmon Strait lies between Kyushu and Honshu.

Kyushu has many volcanoes, hot springs, and beautifully scenic coastlines.

There are eight prefectures in Kyushu, including Okinawa.

Fukuoka City and Kitakyushu City are the two largest megacities in Kyushu, both located in Fukuoka Prefecture.

Transportation in Kyushu

Kyushu can be reached from Tokyo by Shinkansen bullet train. The trip takes about five hours.

In 2011, the Shinkansen line was extended to Kagoshima, the southernmost prefecture in Kyushu.

It takes 1.5 hours to fly from Tokyo to Kyushu.

Because of its proximity to the continent, Kyushu has been the gateway to Japan for centuries.

九州の歴史

□特に古代において、中国や韓国からの無数の技術、文化が、九州経由で日本に入ってきました。

□過去、九州は韓国と多くの交流を行ってきました。

□九州が、日本史の起源と考える人も多いです。

□九州には、先史時代からの考古学的な遺跡が無数にあります。

□封建時代、九州は強力な大名によって分割されていました。例えば、島津氏は現在の鹿児島県を支配していました。

□日本が江戸時代に鎖国をしている間、長崎の出島と呼ばれる人工島が唯一の開かれた港で、オランダ商人だけが、ここで貿易することができました。

□西部九州はその昔、キリスト教が幕府によって禁止されていたとき、隠れキリシタンがいたところとして知られています。

□幕府によってキリスト教が禁止されていた頃、隠れてキリスト教を信仰していた人を、隠れキリシタンといいます。

□隠れてキリスト教を信仰した人の多くが、17世紀、長崎県や熊本県で殉教しました。

福岡県

□福岡県は九州の北端に位置し、県庁所在地は福岡市です。

□九州最大の都市は福岡市で、九州の北部沿岸に位置しています。

□福岡市は九州の商業の中心です。

□福岡空港からは、アジア各地へ飛行機で行くことができます。

□福岡と韓国の釜山の間には、フェリーが運行しています。

History of Kyushu

Especially in ancient times, countless technologies and cultures from China and Korea entered Japan via Kyushu.

In the past, Kyushu had many interactions with Korea.

Many consider Kyushu to be the birthplace of Japanese history.

There are countless archaeological sites in Kyushu dating back to prehistoric times.

During the feudal era, Kyushu was divided by powerful feudal lords. For example, the Shimazu clan ruled what is now Kagoshima Prefecture.

When Japan was isolated during the Edo period (1603-1867), a man-made island called Dejima in Nagasaki was the only open port, and only Dutch merchants could trade there.

Western Kyushu is known as the place where hidden Christians lived when Christianity was banned by the shogunate in the past.

When Christianity was banned by the shogunate, those who believed in Christianity secretly were called "hidden Christians."

Many of those who secretly believed in Christianity were martyred in Nagasaki and Kumamoto Prefectures in the 17th century.

Fukuoka Prefecture

Fukuoka Prefecture is located on the northern tip of Kyushu, and its capital is Fukuoka City.

The largest city in Kyushu is Fukuoka City, which is located on the northern coast of Kyushu.

Fukuoka City is the commercial center of Kyushu.

From Fukuoka Airport, it is possible to fly to many parts of Asia.

There is a ferry service between Fukuoka and Busan, South Korea.

□ 福岡市の下町、博多には地元気質や伝統が残っています。

□ 博多は福岡市の商業地域で、山笠という夏祭りもここで行われます。

水郷の町を流れる柳川

□ 博多山笠は、勢いのいい元気な祭りとして知られています。装飾の施された山車を担ぎ、通りに勢いよく出ていきます。

□ 北九州市はかつて町の南部に炭鉱があったおかげで、鉄鋼業で栄えました。

□ 北九州市は本州から九州への玄関口で、本州の下関とはトンネルと橋でつながっています。

佐賀県

□ 佐賀は、福岡県と長崎県に挟まれた県です。県庁所在地は佐賀市です。

□ 佐賀は伝統的な陶磁器で有名です。伊万里、唐津、有田市などでたくさんの陶磁器が作られています。

□ 佐賀南部は有明海の湾に面しています。湾の干潟にはムツゴロウというひょうきんな魚が生息します。

弥生時代の集落跡、吉野ケ里遺跡

□ 佐賀県北部では、リアス式海岸に沿って素晴らしい景色が堪能できます。

長崎県

□ 長崎は九州の西の端に位置しています。

□ 長崎市は1945年に2発目の原爆が落とされた町です。

□ 広島市と同様、長崎市も平和貢献都市になりました。

□ 封建時代、長崎は日本で海外に開かれた唯一の窓でした。

Hakata, the downtown area of Fukuoka City, retains its local character and traditions.

Hakata is the commercial district of Fukuoka City, and the Yamakasa summer festival is also held here.

Hakata Gion Yamakasa is known as a lively and energetic festival. Decorated floats are carried out into the streets with great energy and enthusiasm.

Kitakyushu City once prospered in the steel industry thanks to the coal mines in the southern part of the city.

Kitakyushu is the gateway to Kyushu from Honshu, and is connected to Shimonoseki in Honshu by a tunnel and bridge.

Saga Prefecture

Saga is located between Fukuoka and Nagasaki prefectures. The prefectural capital is Saga City.

Saga is famous for its traditional ceramics. Many ceramics are produced in Imari, Karatsu, and Arita City.

The southern part of Saga faces the Ariake Sea bay. The mud flats of the bay are inhabited by peculiar fish called *mutsugoro* (mudskipper).

In the northern part of Saga Prefecture, visitors can enjoy wonderful scenery along the ria coast.

Nagasaki Prefecture

Nagasaki is located on the western edge of Kyushu.

Nagasaki is the city where the second atomic bomb was dropped in 1945.

Like Hiroshima, Nagasaki has become a city that contributes to world peace.

During the feudal era, Nagasaki was Japan's only window to the rest of the world.

□ 長崎にはチャイナタウンがあり、そこでは和食と中華を融合させた伝統の料理が楽しめます。

□ チャンポンは長崎に住む中国人が作り出した麺料理です。

□ 長崎県の西岸に沿って、数えきれない島や入り江があります。

重要文化財の頭ケ島天主堂

□ 平戸は歴史的な街で、禁教にも関わらず、ひそかに信仰を続けた隠れキリシタンについて知ることができます。

□ 島原半島には雲仙岳という火山があります。島原市はこの半島にある美しい城下町です。

□ 長崎県の東シナ海には、島々が点在しています。

熊本県

□ 熊本は福岡の南にある県で、県庁所在地は熊本市です。熊本市は熊本城で有名です。

□ 阿蘇山は熊本県にある火山で、九州の真ん中に位置しています。

□ 熊本県西岸には、天草諸島という景色のよい島々が点在しています。

茶臼山上に建てられた熊本城（1607 年）

Nagasaki's Chinatown offers a unique culinary experience, blending Japanese and Chinese flavors in traditional dishes.

Champon is a noodle dish created by the Chinese living in Nagasaki.

Along the western coast of Nagasaki are countless islands and coves.

Hirado is a historical city where visitors can learn about the hidden Christians who secretly continued their faith despite its prohibition.

On the Shimabara Peninsula is a volcano called Mount Unzen. Shimabara City is a beautiful castle town on this peninsula.

Nagasaki Prefecture is dotted with islands in the East China Sea.

Kumamoto Prefecture

Kumamoto is a prefecture located south of Fukuoka, and its capital is Kumamoto City. Kumamoto City is famous for Kumamoto Castle.

Mount Aso is a volcano located in Kumamoto Prefecture, in the middle of Kyushu.

The Amakusa Islands, a group of scenic islands, dot the western coast of Kumamoto Prefecture.

大分県

別府地獄めぐりのひとつ、海地獄

□ 大分県は熊本県の東に位置し、山やリアス式海岸が見事な景観を作り出しています。県庁所在地は大分市です。

□ 大分県の別府と湯布院は、温泉地として有名で、その他、山間部にもたくさんの温泉があります。

□ 国東(くにさき)半島の谷あいにはたくさんの仏教寺院があり、修行の場として知られています。

□ 大分県の宇佐という街には宇佐八幡宮があり、そこは武人の守り神とされています。

宮崎県

特別天然記念物の蘇鉄

□ 宮崎県は九州の南東にあり、黒潮が流れていることで気候はとても温暖です。県庁所在地は宮崎市です。

□ 高千穂は、日本統治のためにニニギノミコトが降臨した場所と言われています。

□ 日南海岸は太平洋に面した人気の観光地です。

鹿児島県

□ 鹿児島県は九州の南部に位置し、県庁所在地は鹿児島市です。

□ 鹿児島湾には桜島があり、活火山です。この火山は鹿児島市の向かい側にあります。

Oita Prefecture

Oita Prefecture is located to the east of Kumamoto Prefecture, and its mountains and ria coastline create a magnificent landscape. The prefectural capital is Oita City.

Beppu and Yufuin in Oita Prefecture are famous for their hot springs, and there are many other hot springs in the mountainous areas.

There are many Buddhist temples in the valleys of the Kunisaki Peninsula, which are known as places of ascetic practice.

In the city of Usa in Oita Prefecture, there is Usa Hachiman Shrine, whose god is considered to be the guardian deity of warriors.

Miyazaki Prefecture

Miyazaki Prefecture is located in the southeast of Kyushu and has a very mild climate due to the Kuroshio Current. The prefectural capital is Miyazaki City.

Takachiho is said to be the place where Niniginomikoto descended to rule Japan.

The Nichinan Coast is a popular tourist destination facing the Pacific Ocean.

Kagoshima Prefecture

Kagoshima Prefecture is located in the southern part of Kyushu, and its capital is Kagoshima City.

In Kagoshima Bay is Sakurajima, an active volcano. This volcano is located across from Kagoshima City.

現在も噴火を繰り返す桜島

□ 霧島は鹿児島にあるもう一つの活火山で、県北部に位置しています。周囲には多くの温泉地があります。

□ 封建時代、鹿児島は薩摩と呼ばれ、島津氏が統治する強力な藩でした。

□ 鹿児島の人々は、鹿児島弁という方言を使っています。

□ 鹿児島県には自然のすばらしい奄美諸島もあります。

□ 種子島は、JAXA（宇宙航空研究開発機構）が運営する宇宙センターがあることで知られています。

沖縄県

□ 沖縄も九州の一部ですが、歴史的にも文化的にもまったく異なります。

□ 沖縄は九州と台湾の間に位置しています。

□ 沖縄県は、亜熱帯気候に属しています。

□ 沖縄は、160の島が連なる南西諸島の南にあり、その県庁所在地は那覇市です。

□ 沖縄県の属する南西諸島を琉球諸島とよびます。

象の鼻の形が特徴的な万座毛

□ 沖縄は熱帯の自然があり、日本人にとって人気の観光地です。

□ 沖縄の文化やライフスタイルは、その位置、歴史的背景により、ほかの日本の地域とはまったく異なっています。

□ 沖縄独自の料理、酒、そしてタバコがあります。

□ 島唄と呼ばれる沖縄の民謡が、歌い継がれています。

Kirishima is another active volcano in Kagoshima and is located in the northern part of the prefecture. There are many hot spring resorts in the surrounding area.

In feudal times, Kagoshima was known as Satsuma, a powerful domain ruled by the Shimazu clan.

The people of Kagoshima use a dialect called *Kagoshima-ben*.

Kagoshima Prefecture is also home to the beautiful Amami Islands, a natural wonder.

Tanegashima Island is known for its space center operated by the Japan Aerospace Exploration Agency (JAXA).

Okinawa Prefecture

Okinawa is also part of Kyushu, but historically and culturally, it is quite different.

Okinawa is located between Kyushu and Taiwan.

Okinawa Prefecture has a subtropical climate.

Okinawa is located in the south of the Nansei Islands, a chain of 160 islands, and its capital is Naha City.

Parts of the southwestern islands, to which Okinawa Prefecture belongs, are called the Ryukyu Islands.

Okinawa's tropical nature makes it a popular tourist destination for the Japanese.

Due to its location and historical background, the culture and lifestyle of Okinawa are quite different from the rest of Japan.

Okinawa has its own unique cuisine, sake, and cigarettes.

Okinawan folk songs, called *shimauta*, are sung and passed down from generation to generation.

□ 島唄は沖縄の民謡で、地元の弦楽器である三線にあわせて歌われます。

□ 三線は蛇皮線とも呼ばれます。三線は沖縄独特の楽器で、弦が3本で、胴の部分には蛇の皮が張られています。

□ 沖縄はかつては琉球王国という独立国でした。

□ 琉球王国のグスク、および関連遺産はユネスコの世界遺産に登録されています。

□ 17世紀、日本による侵攻が始まりました。

□ 沖縄が公式に日本となったのは1879年のことです。

□ 1945年、沖縄はアメリカ軍に攻撃され、激しい戦場となりました。

□ 沖縄の戦闘で、9万4000人以上の人が亡くなり、その多くが市民でした。

□ 戦争中、看護師として従軍していた多くの若い女学生が殺されたり、自殺したりした壕が、沖縄南端にあります。

□ 沖縄戦の被害者には看護師として従軍していた若い女学生もいました。彼女たちはひめゆり部隊として知られています。

□ 沖縄は第二次世界大戦中、国内最大の地上戦が行われた県です。

□ 日米安全保障条約により、沖縄本島にはたくさんの米軍基地があります。

□ 日本人にとって、沖縄本島の約15%を占める米軍基地の問題は、賛否両論ある政治的関心事です。

Shimauta are Okinawan folk songs sung to the accompaniment of the local stringed instrument, the *sanshin*.

The *sanshin* is also called a *jabisen*. The *sanshin* is a uniquely Okinawan instrument with three strings and a body covered with snakeskin.

Okinawa was once an independent country called the Ryukyu Kingdom.

The *gusuks* of the Kingdom of the Ryukyus and related heritage sites are listed as a UNESCO World Heritage Site.

In the 17th century, an invasion by Japan began.

Okinawa officially became part of Japan in 1879.

In 1945, Okinawa was attacked by American forces and became the scene of a fierce battle.

More than 94,000 people died in the fighting in Okinawa, many of them civilians.

A bunker where many young female students who served as nurses during the war were killed or committed suicide is located on the southern tip of Okinawa.

Among the victims of the Battle of Okinawa were young female students who served as nurses. They are known as the Himeyuri corps.

Okinawa was the prefecture where the largest ground war in Japan took place during World War II.

Due to the Japan-US Security Treaty, there are many US military bases on the main island of Okinawa.

For Japanese people, the issue of US military bases, which occupy about 15% of the main island of Okinawa, is a politically sensitive topic with arguments both for and against it.

＼ちょこっと／
知っておきたい日本紹介のコツ⑤

● 地方の説明

日本各地を説明するとき、まずその位置について相手に理解してもらわなければなりません。初めて日本に来る人たちは、日本の地理についての知識はあまり持っていないことを前提としましょう。外国人にとって有名な場所として、まずは東京と京都、また被爆地として知られている広島や長崎もあります。こうした場所からの方角や距離によって、まず大まかな位置を理解してもらうことが大切です。そして、歴史的な説明よりは、どこに昔ながらの町並みがあり、お城はどこにあるといった一般的な話から入っていくことをおすすめします。多くの人たちは、観光スポットを通してその町の歴史を知っていきます。本書に登場するフレーズを参考に、自分たちの町を紹介していけるといいですね。

● 外国人が尋ねる政治の問題

日本に関心のある外国の人から、日本の政治について質問されることもあるかもしれません。2011 年に発生した福島第一原発事故の問題や、1955 年から 4 年間を除いてずっと同じ政党が政権を握っている日本の民主主義の奇異さなど、海外メディアで報道される日本の姿は彼らにとって不思議に満ちていることでしょう。こうした質問に対しては、自分の意見を明快に解説できるように、普段から心がけたいものです。

外国の人とは、政治的な会話はよほど親しくならない限り、慎んだほうが良いとよく言われます。しかし、彼らにとって外国である日本の政治情勢について話をすることは問題ありません。特に、相手が関心をもっている話題である以上、今の日本の課題について、しっかりと説明することは必要なことでしょう。

English Conversational Ability Test
国際英語会話能力検定

● E-CATとは…
英語が話せるようになるためのテストです。インターネットベースで、30分であなたの発話力をチェックします。

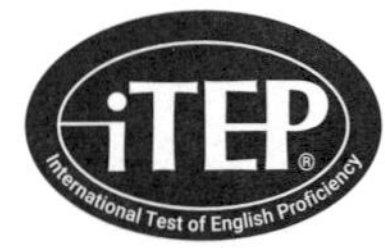

● iTEP®とは…
世界各国の企業、政府機関、アメリカの大学300校以上が、英語能力判定テストとして採用。オンラインによる90分のテストで文法、リーディング、リスニング、ライティング、スピーキングの5技能をスコア化。iTEP®は、留学、就職、海外赴任などに必要な、世界に通用する英語力を総合的に評価する画期的なテストです。

www.itepexamjapan.com

英語 日本紹介事典 JAPAPEDIA（ジャパペディア）［新版］

2024年 7 月11日　第1刷発行

編　　者　IBCパブリッシング

発 行 者　賀川　洋

発 行 所　IBCパブリッシング株式会社
〒162-0804 東京都新宿区中里町29番3号 菱秀神楽坂ビル
Tel. 03-3513-4511　Fax. 03-3513-4512
www.ibcpub.co.jp

印 刷 所　株式会社シナノパブリッシングプレス

© IBC Publishing 2024

Printed in Japan

落丁本・乱丁本は、小社宛にお送りください。送料小社負担にてお取り替えいたします。
本書の無断複写（コピー）は著作権法上での例外を除き禁じられています。

ISBN978-4-7946-0821-5